T0145809

Sword Blades and Poppy Seed

Sword Blades and Poppy Seed

Amy Lowell

MINT EDITIONS

Sword Blades and Poppy Seed was first published in 1914.

This edition published by Mint Editions 2021.

ISBN 9781513295862 | E-ISBN 9781513297361

Published by Mint Editions®

 MINT
EDITIONS
minteditionbooks.com

Publishing Director: Jennifer Newens
Design & Production: Rachel Lopez Metzger
Project Manager: Micaela Clark
Typesetting: Westchester Publishing Services

Contents

Preface

No one expects a man to make a chair without first learning how, but there is a popular impression that the poet is born, not made, and that his verses burst from his overflowing heart of themselves. As a matter of fact, the poet must learn his trade in the same manner, and with the same painstaking care, as the cabinet-maker. His heart may overflow with high thoughts and sparkling fancies, but if he cannot convey them to his reader by means of the written word he has no claim to be considered a poet. A workman may be pardoned, therefore, for spending a few moments to explain and describe the technique of his trade. A work of beauty which cannot stand an intimate examination is a poor and jerry-built thing.

In the first place, I wish to state my firm belief that poetry should not try to teach, that it should exist simply because it is a created beauty, even if sometimes the beauty of a gothic grotesque. We do not ask the trees to teach us moral lessons, and only the Salvation Army feels it necessary to pin texts upon them. We know that these texts are ridiculous, but many of us do not yet see that to write an obvious moral all over a work of art, picture, statue, or poem, is not only ridiculous, but timid and vulgar. We distrust a beauty we only half understand, and rush in with our impertinent suggestions. How far we are from "admitting the Universe"! The Universe, which flings down its continents and seas, and leaves them without comment. Art is as much a function of the Universe as an Equinoctial gale, or the Law of Gravitation; and we insist upon considering it merely a little scroll-work, of no great importance unless it be studded with nails from which pretty and uplifting sentiments may be hung!

For the purely technical side I must state my immense debt to the French, and perhaps above all to the, so-called, Parnassian School, although some of the writers who have influenced me most do not belong to it. High-minded and untiring workmen, they have spared no pains to produce a poetry finer than that of any other country in our time. Poetry so full of beauty and feeling, that the study of it is at once an inspiration and a despair to the artist. The Anglo-Saxon of our day has a tendency to think that a fine idea excuses slovenly workmanship. These clear-eyed Frenchmen are a reproof to our self-satisfied laziness. Before the works of Parnassians like Leconte de Lisle, and José-Maria de Heredia, or those of Henri de Régnier, Albert Samain, Francis Jammes, Remy de Gourmont, and Paul Fort, of the more modern school, we stand rebuked. Indeed—"They order this matter better in France."

It is because in France, today, poetry is so living and vigorous a thing, that so many metrical experiments come from there. Only a vigorous tree has the vitality to put forth new branches. The poet with originality and power is always seeking to give his readers the same poignant feeling which he has himself. To do this he must constantly find new and striking images, delightful and unexpected forms. Take the word "daybreak," for instance. What a remarkable picture it must once have conjured up! The great, round sun, like the yolk of some mighty egg, BREAKING through cracked and splintered clouds. But we have said "daybreak" so often that we do not see the picture any more, it has become only another word for dawn. The poet must be constantly seeking new pictures to make his readers feel the vitality of his thought.

Many of the poems in this volume are written in what the French call "Vers Libre," a nomenclature more suited to French use and to French versification than to ours. I prefer to call them poems in "unrhymed cadence," for that conveys their exact meaning to an English ear. They are built upon "organic rhythm," or the rhythm of the speaking voice with its necessity for breathing, rather than upon a strict metrical system. They differ from ordinary prose rhythms by being more curved, and containing more stress. The stress, and exceedingly marked curve, of any regular metre is easily perceived. These poems, built upon cadence, are more subtle, but the laws they follow are not less fixed. Merely chopping prose lines into lengths does not produce cadence, it is constructed upon mathematical and absolute laws of balance and time. In the preface to his "Poems," Henley speaks of "those unrhyming rhythms in which I had tried to quintessentialize, as (I believe) one scarce can do in rhyme." The desire to "quintessentialize," to head-up an emotion until it burns white-hot, seems to be an integral part of the modern temper, and certainly "unrhymed cadence" is unique in its power of expressing this.

Three of these poems are written in a form which, so far as I know, has never before been attempted in English. M. Paul Fort is its inventor, and the results it has yielded to him are most beautiful and satisfactory. Perhaps it is more suited to the French language than to English. But I found it the only medium in which these particular poems could be written. It is a fluid and changing form, now prose, now verse, and permitting a great variety of treatment.

But the reader will see that I have not entirely abandoned the more classic English metres. I cannot see why, because certain manners suit certain emotions and subjects, it should be considered imperative for an author to employ no others. Schools are for those who can confine themselves within them. Perhaps it is a weakness in me that I cannot.

In conclusion, I would say that these remarks are in answer to many questions asked me by people who have happened to read some of these poems in periodicals. They are not for the purpose of forestalling criticism, nor of courting it; and they deal, as I said in the beginning, solely with the question of technique. For the more important part of the book, the poems must speak for themselves.

Amy Lowell
May 19, 1914

SWORD BLADES AND POPPY SEED

A drifting, April, twilight sky,
A wind which blew the puddles dry,
And slapped the river into waves
That ran and hid among the staves
Of an old wharf. A watery light
Touched bleak the granite bridge, and white
Without the slightest tinge of gold,
The city shivered in the cold.
All day my thoughts had lain as dead,
Unborn and bursting in my head.
From time to time I wrote a word
Which lines and circles overscored.
My table seemed a graveyard, full
Of coffins waiting burial.
I seized these vile abortions, tore
Them into jagged bits, and swore
To be the dupe of hope no more.
Into the evening straight I went,
Starved of a day's accomplishment.
Unnoticing, I wandered where
The city gave a space for air,
And on the bridge's parapet
I leant, while pallidly there set
A dim, discouraged, worn-out sun.
Behind me, where the tramways run,
Blossomed bright lights, I turned to leave,
When someone plucked me by the sleeve.
"Your pardon, Sir, but I should be
Most grateful could you lend to me
A carfare, I have lost my purse."
The voice was clear, concise, and terse.
I turned and met the quiet gaze
Of strange eyes flashing through the haze.

The man was old and slightly bent,
Under his cloak some instrument
Disarranged its stately line,
He rested on his cane a fine
And nervous hand, an almandine

Smouldered with dull-red flames, sanguine
It burned in twisted gold, upon
His finger. Like some Spanish don,
Conferring favours even when
Asking an alms, he bowed again
And waited. But my pockets proved
Empty, in vain I poked and shoved,
No hidden penny lurking there
Greeted my search. "Sir, I declare
I have no money, pray forgive,
But let me take you where you live."
And so we plodded through the mire
Where street lamps cast a wavering fire.
I took no note of where we went,
His talk became the element
Wherein my being swam, content.
It flashed like rapiers in the night
Lit by uncertain candle-light,
When on some moon-forsaken sward
A quarrel dies upon a sword.
It hacked and carved like a cutlass blade,
And the noise in the air the broad words made
Was the cry of the wind at a window-pane
On an Autumn night of sobbing rain.
Then it would run like a steady stream
Under pinnacled bridges where minarets gleam,
Or lap the air like the lapping tide
Where a marble staircase lifts its wide
Green-spotted steps to a garden gate,
And a waning moon is sinking straight
Down to a black and ominous sea,
While a nightingale sings in a lemon tree.

I walked as though some opiate
Had stung and dulled my brain, a state
Acute and slumbrous. It grew late.
We stopped, a house stood silent, dark.
The old man scratched a match, the spark
Lit up the keyhole of a door,

We entered straight upon a floor
White with finest powdered sand
Carefully sifted, one might stand
Muddy and dripping, and yet no trace
Would stain the boards of this kitchen-place.
From the chimney, red eyes sparked the gloom,
And a cricket's chirp filled all the room.
My host threw pine-cones on the fire
And crimson and scarlet glowed the pyre
Wrapped in the golden flame's desire.
The chamber opened like an eye,
As a half-melted cloud in a Summer sky
The soul of the house stood guessed, and shy
It peered at the stranger warily.
A little shop with its various ware
Spread on shelves with nicest care.
Pitchers, and jars, and jugs, and pots,
Pipkins, and mugs, and many lots
Of lacquered canisters, black and gold,
Like those in which Chinese tea is sold.
Chests, and puncheons, kegs, and flasks,
Goblets, chalices, firkins, and casks.
In a corner three ancient amphorae leaned
Against the wall, like ships careened.
There was dusky blue of Wedgewood ware,
The carved, white figures fluttering there
Like leaves adrift upon the air.
Classic in touch, but emasculate,
The Greek soul grown effeminate.
The factory of Sevres had lent
Elegant boxes with ornament
Culled from gardens where fountains splashed
And golden carp in the shadows flashed,
Nuzzling for crumbs under lily-pads,
Which ladies threw as the last of fads.
Eggshell trays where gay beaux knelt,
Hand on heart, and daintily spelt
Their love in flowers, brittle and bright,
Artificial and fragile, which told aright

The vows of an eighteenth-century knight.
The cruder tones of old Dutch jugs
Glared from one shelf, where Toby mugs
Endlessly drank the foaming ale,
Its froth grown dusty, awaiting sale.
The glancing light of the burning wood
Played over a group of jars which stood
On a distant shelf, it seemed the sky
Had lent the half-tones of his blazonry
To paint these porcelains with unknown hues
Of reds dyed purple and greens turned blues,
Of lustres with so evanescent a sheen
Their colours are felt, but never seen.
Strange winged dragons writhe about
These vases, poisoned venoms spout,
Impregnate with old Chinese charms;
Sealed urns containing mortal harms,
They fill the mind with thoughts impure,
Pestilent drippings from the ure
Of vicious thinkings. "Ah, I see,"
Said I, "you deal in pottery."
The old man turned and looked at me.
Shook his head gently. "No," said he.

Then from under his cloak he took the thing
Which I had wondered to see him bring
Guarded so carefully from sight.
As he laid it down it flashed in the light,
A Toledo blade, with basket hilt,
Damascened with arabesques of gilt,
Or rather gold, and tempered so
It could cut a floating thread at a blow.
The old man smiled, "It has no sheath,
'Twas a little careless to have it beneath
My cloak, for a jostle to my arm
Would have resulted in serious harm.
But it was so fine, I could not wait,
So I brought it with me despite its state."
"An amateur of arms," I thought,

AMY LOWELL

"Bringing home a prize which he has bought."
"You care for this sort of thing, Dear Sir?"
"Not in the way which you infer.
I need them in business, that is all."
And he pointed his finger at the wall.
Then I saw what I had not noticed before.
The walls were hung with at least five score
Of swords and daggers of every size
Which nations of militant men could devise.
Poisoned spears from tropic seas,
That natives, under banana trees,
Smear with the juice of some deadly snake.
Blood-dipped arrows, which savages make
And tip with feathers, orange and green,
A quivering death, in harlequin sheen.
High up, a fan of glancing steel
Was formed of claymores in a wheel.
Jewelled swords worn at kings' levees
Were suspended next midshipmen's dirks, and these
Elbowed stilettos come from Spain,
Chased with some splendid Hidalgo's name.
There were Samurai swords from old Japan,
And scimitars from Hindoostan,
While the blade of a Turkish yataghan
Made a waving streak of vitreous white
Upon the wall, in the firelight.
Foils with buttons broken or lost
Lay heaped on a chair, among them tossed
The boarding-pike of a privateer.
Against the chimney leaned a queer
Two-handed weapon, with edges dull
As though from hacking on a skull.
The rusted blood corroded it still.
My host took up a paper spill
From a heap which lay in an earthen bowl,
And lighted it at a burning coal.
At either end of the table, tall
Wax candles were placed, each in a small,
And slim, and burnished candlestick

Of pewter. The old man lit each wick,
And the room leapt more obviously
Upon my mind, and I could see
What the flickering fire had hid from me.
Above the chimney's yawning throat,
Shoulder high, like the dark wainscote,
Was a mantelshelf of polished oak
Blackened with the pungent smoke
Of firelit nights; a Cromwell clock
Of tarnished brass stood like a rock
In the midst of a heaving, turbulent sea
Of every sort of cutlery.
There lay knives sharpened to any use,
The keenest lancet, and the obtuse
And blunted pruning bill-hook; blades
Of razors, scalpels, shears; cascades
Of penknives, with handles of mother-of-pearl,
And scythes, and sickles, and scissors; a whirl
Of points and edges, and underneath
Shot the gleam of a saw with bristling teeth.
My head grew dizzy, I seemed to hear
A battle-cry from somewhere near,
The clash of arms, and the squeal of balls,
And the echoless thud when a dead man falls.
A smoky cloud had veiled the room,
Shot through with lurid glares; the gloom
Pounded with shouts and dying groans,
With the drip of blood on cold, hard stones.
Sabres and lances in streaks of light
Gleamed through the smoke, and at my right
A creese, like a licking serpent's tongue,
Glittered an instant, while it stung.
Streams, and points, and lines of fire!
The livid steel, which man's desire
Had forged and welded, burned white and cold.
Every blade which man could mould,
Which could cut, or slash, or cleave, or rip,
Or pierce, or thrust, or carve, or strip,
Or gash, or chop, or puncture, or tear,

Or slice, or hack, they all were there.
Nerveless and shaking, round and round,
I stared at the walls and at the ground,
Till the room spun like a whipping top,
And a stern voice in my ear said, "Stop!
I sell no tools for murderers here.
Of what are you thinking! Please clear
Your mind of such imaginings.
Sit down. I will tell you of these things."

He pushed me into a great chair
Of russet leather, poked a flare
Of tumbling flame, with the old long sword,
Up the chimney; but said no word.
Slowly he walked to a distant shelf,
And brought back a crock of finest delf.
He rested a moment a blue-veined hand
Upon the cover, then cut a band
Of paper, pasted neatly round,
Opened and poured. A sliding sound
Came from beneath his old white hands,
And I saw a little heap of sands,
Black and smooth. What could they be:
"Pepper," I thought. He looked at me.
"What you see is poppy seed.
Lethean dreams for those in need."
He took up the grains with a gentle hand
And sifted them slowly like hour-glass sand.
On his old white finger the almandine
Shot out its rays, incarnadine.
"Visions for those too tired to sleep.
These seeds cast a film over eyes which weep.
No single soul in the world could dwell,
Without these poppy-seeds I sell."
For a moment he played with the shining stuff,
Passing it through his fingers. Enough
At last, he poured it back into
The china jar of Holland blue,
Which he carefully carried to its place.

Then, with a smile on his aged face,
He drew up a chair to the open space
'Twixt table and chimney. "Without preface,
Young man, I will say that what you see
Is not the puzzle you take it to be."
"But surely, Sir, there is something strange
In a shop with goods at so wide a range
Each from the other, as swords and seeds.
Your neighbours must have greatly differing needs."
"My neighbours," he said, and he stroked his chin,
"Live everywhere from here to Pekin.
But you are wrong, my sort of goods
Is but one thing in all its moods."
He took a shagreen letter case
From his pocket, and with charming grace
Offered me a printed card.
I read the legend, "Ephraim Bard.
Dealer in Words." And that was all.
I stared at the letters, whimsical
Indeed, or was it merely a jest.
He answered my unasked request:
"All books are either dreams or swords,
You can cut, or you can drug, with words.
My firm is a very ancient house,
The entries on my books would rouse
Your wonder, perhaps incredulity.
I inherited from an ancestry
Stretching remotely back and far,
This business, and my clients are
As were those of my grandfather's days,
Writers of books, and poems, and plays.
My swords are tempered for every speech,
For fencing wit, or to carve a breach
Through old abuses the world condones.
In another room are my grindstones and hones,
For whetting razors and putting a point
On daggers, sometimes I even anoint
The blades with a subtle poison, so
A twofold result may follow the blow.

These are purchased by men who feel
The need of stabbing society's heel,
Which egotism has brought them to think
Is set on their necks. I have foils to pink
An adversary to quaint reply,
And I have customers who buy
Scalpels with which to dissect the brains
And hearts of men. Ultramundanes
Even demand some finer kinds
To open their own souls and minds.
But the other half of my business deals
With visions and fancies. Under seals,
Sorted, and placed in vessels here,
I keep the seeds of an atmosphere.
Each jar contains a different kind
Of poppy seed. From farthest Ind
Come the purple flowers, opium filled,
From which the weirdest myths are distilled;
My orient porcelains contain them all.
Those Lowestoft pitchers against the wall
Hold a lighter kind of bright conceit;
And those old Saxe vases, out of the heat
On that lowest shelf beside the door,
Have a sort of Ideal, "couleur d'or."
Every castle of the air
Sleeps in the fine black grains, and there
Are seeds for every romance, or light
Whiff of a dream for a summer night.
I supply to every want and taste."
'Twas slowly said, in no great haste
He seemed to push his wares, but I
Dumfounded listened. By and by
A log on the fire broke in two.
He looked up quickly, "Sir, and you?"
I groped for something I should say;
Amazement held me numb. "Today
You sweated at a fruitless task."
He spoke for me, "What do you ask?
How can I serve you?" "My kind host,

My penniless state was not a boast;
I have no money with me." He smiled.
"Not for that money I beguiled
You here; you paid me in advance."
Again I felt as though a trance
Had dimmed my faculties. Again
He spoke, and this time to explain.
"The money I demand is Life,
Your nervous force, your joy, your strife!"
What infamous proposal now
Was made me with so calm a brow?
Bursting through my lethargy,
Indignantly I hurled the cry:
"Is this a nightmare, or am I
Drunk with some infernal wine?
I am no Faust, and what is mine
Is what I call my soul! Old Man!
Devil or Ghost! Your hellish plan
Revolts me. Let me go." "My child,"
And the old tones were very mild,
"I have no wish to barter souls;
My traffic does not ask such tolls.
I am no devil; is there one?
Surely the age of fear is gone.
We live within a daylight world
Lit by the sun, where winds unfurled
Sweep clouds to scatter pattering rain,
And then blow back the sun again.
I sell my fancies, or my swords,
To those who care far more for words,
Ideas, of which they are the sign,
Than any other life-design.
Who buy of me must simply pay
Their whole existence quite away:
Their strength, their manhood, and their prime,
Their hours from morning till the time
When evening comes on tiptoe feet,
And losing life, think it complete;
Must miss what other men count being,

To gain the gift of deeper seeing;
Must spurn all ease, all hindering love,
All which could hold or bind; must prove
The farthest boundaries of thought,
And shun no end which these have brought;
Then die in satisfaction, knowing
That what was sown was worth the sowing.
I claim for all the goods I sell
That they will serve their purpose well,
And though you perish, they will live.
Full measure for your pay I give.
Today you worked, you thought, in vain.
What since has happened is the train
Your toiling brought. I spoke to you
For my share of the bargain, due."
"My life! And is that all you crave
In pay? What even childhood gave!
I have been dedicate from youth.
Before my God I speak the truth!"
Fatigue, excitement of the past
Few hours broke me down at last.
All day I had forgot to eat,
My nerves betrayed me, lacking meat.
I bowed my head and felt the storm
Plough shattering through my prostrate form.
The tearless sobs tore at my heart.
My host withdrew himself apart;
Busied among his crockery,
He paid no farther heed to me.
Exhausted, spent, I huddled there,
Within the arms of the old carved chair.

A long half-hour dragged away,
And then I heard a kind voice say,
"The day will soon be dawning, when
You must begin to work again.
Here are the things which you require."
By the fading light of the dying fire,
And by the guttering candle's flare,

I saw the old man standing there.
He handed me a packet, tied
With crimson tape, and sealed. "Inside
Are seeds of many differing flowers,
To occupy your utmost powers
Of storied vision, and these swords
Are the finest which my shop affords.
Go home and use them; do not spare
Yourself; let that be all your care.
Whatever you have means to buy
Be very sure I can supply."
He slowly walked to the window, flung
It open, and in the grey air rung
The sound of distant matin bells.
I took my parcels. Then, as tells
An ancient mumbling monk his beads,
I tried to thank for his courteous deeds
My strange old friend. "Nay, do not talk,"
He urged me, "you have a long walk
Before you. Good-bye and Good-day!"
And gently sped upon my way
I stumbled out in the morning hush,
As down the empty street a flush
Ran level from the rising sun.
Another day was just begun.

SWORD BLADES

THE CAPTURED GODDESS

Over the housetops,
Above the rotating chimney-pots,
I have seen a shiver of amethyst,
And blue and cinnamon have flickered
A moment,
At the far end of a dusty street.

Through sheeted rain
Has come a lustre of crimson,
And I have watched moonbeams
Hushed by a film of palest green.

It was her wings,
Goddess!
Who stepped over the clouds,
And laid her rainbow feathers
Aslant on the currents of the air.

I followed her for long,
With gazing eyes and stumbling feet.
I cared not where she led me,
My eyes were full of colours:
Saffrons, rubies, the yellows of beryls,
And the indigo-blue of quartz;
Flights of rose, layers of chrysoprase,
Points of orange, spirals of vermilion,
The spotted gold of tiger-lily petals,
The loud pink of bursting hydrangeas.
I followed,
And watched for the flashing of her wings.

In the city I found her,
The narrow-streeted city.
In the market-place I came upon her,
Bound and trembling.
Her fluted wings were fastened to her sides with cords,

She was naked and cold,
For that day the wind blew
Without sunshine.

Men chaffered for her,
They bargained in silver and gold,
In copper, in wheat,
And called their bids across the market-place.

The Goddess wept.

Hiding my face I fled,
And the grey wind hissed behind me,
Along the narrow streets.

The Precinct. Rochester

The tall yellow hollyhocks stand,
 Still and straight,
With their round blossoms spread open,
In the quiet sunshine.
And still is the old Roman wall,
Rough with jagged bits of flint,
And jutting stones,
Old and cragged,
Quite still in its antiquity.
The pear-trees press their branches against it,
And feeling it warm and kindly,
The little pears ripen to yellow and red.
They hang heavy, bursting with juice,
Against the wall.
So old, so still!

The sky is still.
The clouds make no sound
As they slide away
Beyond the Cathedral Tower,
To the river,
And the sea.
It is very quiet,
Very sunny.
The myrtle flowers stretch themselves in the sunshine,
But make no sound.
The roses push their little tendrils up,
And climb higher and higher.
In spots they have climbed over the wall.
But they are very still,
They do not seem to move.
And the old wall carries them
Without effort, and quietly
Ripens and shields the vines and blossoms.

A bird in a plane-tree
Sings a few notes,
Cadenced and perfect
They weave into the silence.
The Cathedral bell knocks,
One, two, three, and again,
And then again.
It is a quiet sound,
Calling to prayer,
Hardly scattering the stillness,
Only making it close in more densely.
The gardener picks ripe gooseberries
For the Dean's supper tonight.
It is very quiet,
Very regulated and mellow.
But the wall is old,
It has known many days.
It is a Roman wall,
Left-over and forgotten.

Beyond the Cathedral Close
Yelp and mutter the discontents of people not mellow,
Not well-regulated.
People who care more for bread than for beauty,
Who would break the tombs of saints,
And give the painted windows of churches
To their children for toys.
People who say:
"They are dead, we live!
The world is for the living."

Fools! It is always the dead who breed.
Crush the ripe fruit, and cast it aside,
Yet its seeds shall fructify,
And trees rise where your huts were standing.
But the little people are ignorant,
They chaffer, and swarm.
They gnaw like rats,
And the foundations of the Cathedral are honeycombed.

AMY LOWELL

The Dean is in the Chapter House;
He is reading the architect's bill
For the completed restoration of the Cathedral.
He will have ripe gooseberries for supper,
And then he will walk up and down the path
By the wall,
And admire the snapdragons and dahlias,
Thinking how quiet and peaceful
The garden is.
The old wall will watch him,
Very quietly and patiently it will watch.
For the wall is old,
It is a Roman wall.

THE CYCLISTS

Spread on the roadway,
With open-blown jackets,
Like black, soaring pinions,
They swoop down the hillside,
    The Cyclists.

Seeming dark-plumaged
Birds, after carrion,
Careening and circling,
Over the dying
    Of England.

She lies with her bosom
Beneath them, no longer
The Dominant Mother,
The Virile—but rotting
    Before time.

The smell of her, tainted,
Has bitten their nostrils.
Exultant they hover,
And shadow the sun with
    Foreboding.

Sunshine through a Cobwebbed Window

What charm is yours, you faded old-world tapestries,
Of outworn, childish mysteries,
    Vague pageants woven on a web of dream!
    And we, pushing and fighting in the turbid stream
Of modern life, find solace in your tarnished broideries.

Old lichened halls, sun-shaded by huge cedar-trees,
The layered branches horizontal stretched, like Japanese
    Dark-banded prints. Carven cathedrals, on a sky
    Of faintest colour, where the gothic spires fly
And sway like masts, against a shifting breeze.

Worm-eaten pages, clasped in old brown vellum, shrunk
From over-handling, by some anxious monk.
    Or Virgin's Hours, bright with gold and graven
    With flowers, and rare birds, and all the Saints of Heaven,
And Noah's ark stuck on Ararat, when all the world had sunk.

They soothe us like a song, heard in a garden, sung
By youthful minstrels, on the moonlight flung
    In cadences and falls, to ease a queen,
    Widowed and childless, cowering in a screen
Of myrtles, whose life hangs with all its threads unstrung.

A London Thoroughfare. 2 a.m.

They have watered the street,
It shines in the glare of lamps,
Cold, white lamps,
And lies
Like a slow-moving river,
Barred with silver and black.
Cabs go down it,
One,
And then another.
Between them I hear the shuffling of feet.
Tramps doze on the window-ledges,
Night-walkers pass along the sidewalks.
The city is squalid and sinister,
With the silver-barred street in the midst,
Slow-moving,
A river leading nowhere.

Opposite my window,
The moon cuts,
Clear and round,
Through the plum-coloured night.
She cannot light the city;
It is too bright.
It has white lamps,
And glitters coldly.

I stand in the window and watch the moon.
She is thin and lustreless,
But I love her.
I know the moon,
And this is an alien city.

Astigmatism

To Ezra Pound

With much friendship and admiration and
some differences of opinion

The Poet took his walking-stick
Of fine and polished ebony.
Set in the close-grained wood
Were quaint devices;
Patterns in ambers,
And in the clouded green of jades.
The top was of smooth, yellow ivory,
And a tassel of tarnished gold
Hung by a faded cord from a hole
Pierced in the hard wood,
Circled with silver.
For years the Poet had wrought upon this cane.
His wealth had gone to enrich it,
His experiences to pattern it,
His labour to fashion and burnish it.
To him it was perfect,
A work of art and a weapon,
A delight and a defence.
The Poet took his walking-stick
And walked abroad.

Peace be with you, Brother.

The Poet came to a meadow.
Sifted through the grass were daisies,
Open-mouthed, wondering, they gazed at the sun.
The Poet struck them with his cane.
The little heads flew off, and they lay
Dying, open-mouthed and wondering,

On the hard ground.
"They are useless. They are not roses," said the Poet.

Peace be with you, Brother. Go your ways.

The Poet came to a stream.
Purple and blue flags waded in the water;
In among them hopped the speckled frogs;
The wind slid through them, rustling.
The Poet lifted his cane,
And the iris heads fell into the water.
They floated away, torn and drowning.
"Wretched flowers," said the Poet,
"They are not roses."

Peace be with you, Brother. It is your affair.

The Poet came to a garden.
Dahlias ripened against a wall,
Gillyflowers stood up bravely for all their short stature,
And a trumpet-vine covered an arbour
With the red and gold of its blossoms.
Red and gold like the brass notes of trumpets.
The Poet knocked off the stiff heads of the dahlias,
And his cane lopped the gillyflowers at the ground.
Then he severed the trumpet-blossoms from their stems.
Red and gold they lay scattered,
Red and gold, as on a battle field;
Red and gold, prone and dying.
"They were not roses," said the Poet.

Peace be with you, Brother.
But behind you is destruction, and waste places.

The Poet came home at evening,
And in the candle-light

AMY LOWELL

He wiped and polished his cane.
The orange candle flame leaped in the yellow ambers,
And made the jades undulate like green pools.
It played along the bright ebony,
And glowed in the top of cream-coloured ivory.
But these things were dead,
Only the candle-light made them seem to move.
"It is a pity there were no roses," said the Poet.

Peace be with you, Brother. You have chosen your part.

THE COAL PICKER

He perches in the slime, inert,
Bedaubed with iridescent dirt.
The oil upon the puddles dries
To colours like a peacock's eyes,
And half-submerged tomato-cans
Shine scaly, as leviathans
Oozily crawling through the mud.
The ground is here and there bestud
With lumps of only part-burned coal.
His duty is to glean the whole,
To pick them from the filth, each one,
To hoard them for the hidden sun
Which glows within each fiery core
And waits to be made free once more.
Their sharp and glistening edges cut
His stiffened fingers. Through the smut
Gleam red the wounds which will not shut.
Wet through and shivering he kneels
And digs the slippery coals; like eels
They slide about. His force all spent,
He counts his small accomplishment.
A half-a-dozen clinker-coals
Which still have fire in their souls.
Fire! And in his thought there burns
The topaz fire of votive urns.
He sees it fling from hill to hill,
And still consumed, is burning still.
Higher and higher leaps the flame,
The smoke an ever-shifting frame.
He sees a Spanish Castle old,
With silver steps and paths of gold.
From myrtle bowers comes the plash
Of fountains, and the emerald flash
Of parrots in the orange trees,
Whose blossoms pasture humming bees.
He knows he feeds the urns whose smoke

Bears visions, that his master-stroke
Is out of dirt and misery
To light the fire of poesy.
He sees the glory, yet he knows
That others cannot see his shows.
To them his smoke is sightless, black,
His votive vessels but a pack
Of old discarded shards, his fire
A peddler's; still to him the pyre
Is incensed, an enduring goal!
He sighs and grubs another coal.

Storm-Racked

How should I sing when buffeting salt waves
    And stung with bitter surges, in whose might
    I toss, a cockleshell? The dreadful night
Marshals its undefeated dark and raves
In brutal madness, reeling over graves
    Of vanquished men, long-sunken out of sight,
    Sent wailing down to glut the ghoulish sprite
Who haunts foul seaweed forests and their caves.
    No parting cloud reveals a watery star,
My cries are washed away upon the wind,
    My cramped and blistering hands can find no spar,
My eyes with hope o'erstrained, are growing blind.
    But painted on the sky great visions burn,
    My voice, oblation from a shattered urn!

AMY LOWELL

CONVALESCENCE

From out the dragging vastness of the sea,
    Wave-fettered, bound in sinuous, seaweed strands,
    He toils toward the rounding beach, and stands
One moment, white and dripping, silently,
Cut like a cameo in lazuli,
    Then falls, betrayed by shifting shells, and lands
    Prone in the jeering water, and his hands
Clutch for support where no support can be.
    So up, and down, and forward, inch by inch,
He gains upon the shore, where poppies glow
And sandflies dance their little lives away.
    The sucking waves retard, and tighter clinch
The weeds about him, but the land-winds blow,
And in the sky there blooms the sun of May.

PATIENCE

Be patient with you?
    When the stooping sky
Leans down upon the hills
And tenderly, as one who soothing stills
    An anguish, gathers earth to lie
Embraced and girdled. Do the sun-filled men
    Feel patience then?

Be patient with you?
    When the snow-girt earth
Cracks to let through a spurt
Of sudden green, and from the muddy dirt
    A snowdrop leaps, how mark its worth
To eyes frost-hardened, and do weary men
    Feel patience then?

Be patient with you?
    When pain's iron bars
Their rivets tighten, stern
To bend and break their victims; as they turn,
    Hopeless, there stand the purple jars
Of night to spill oblivion. Do these men
    Feel patience then?

Be patient with you?
    You! My sun and moon!
My basketful of flowers!
My money-bag of shining dreams! My hours,
    Windless and still, of afternoon!
You are my world and I your citizen.
    What meaning can have patience then?

Apology

Be not angry with me that I bear
    Your colours everywhere,
    All through each crowded street,
        And meet
    The wonder-light in every eye,
        As I go by.

Each plodding wayfarer looks up to gaze,
    Blinded by rainbow haze,
    The stuff of happiness,
        No less,
    Which wraps me in its glad-hued folds
        Of peacock golds.

Before my feet the dusty, rough-paved way
    Flushes beneath its gray.
    My steps fall ringed with light,
        So bright,
    It seems a myriad suns are strown
        About the town.

Around me is the sound of steepled bells,
    And rich perfumed smells
    Hang like a wind-forgotten cloud,
        And shroud
    Me from close contact with the world.
        I dwell impearled.

You blazon me with jewelled insignia.
    A flaming nebula
    Rims in my life. And yet
        You set
    The word upon me, unconfessed
        To go unguessed.

A Petition

I pray to be the tool which to your hand
    Long use has shaped and moulded till it be
    Apt for your need, and, unconsideringly,
You take it for its service. I demand
To be forgotten in the woven strand
    Which grows the multi-coloured tapestry
    Of your bright life, and through its tissues lie
A hidden, strong, sustaining, grey-toned band.
    I wish to dwell around your daylight dreams,
The railing to the stairway of the clouds,
    To guard your steps securely up, where streams
A faery moonshine washing pale the crowds
    Of pointed stars. Remember not whereby
    You mount, protected, to the far-flung sky.

AMY LOWELL

A BLOCKHEAD

Before me lies a mass of shapeless days,
    Unseparated atoms, and I must
    Sort them apart and live them. Sifted dust
Covers the formless heap. Reprieves, delays,
There are none, ever. As a monk who prays
    The sliding beads asunder, so I thrust
    Each tasteless particle aside, and just
Begin again the task which never stays.
    And I have known a glory of great suns,
When days flashed by, pulsing with joy and fire!
Drunk bubbled wine in goblets of desire,
    And felt the whipped blood laughing as it runs!
Spilt is that liquor, my too hasty hand
Threw down the cup, and did not understand.

STUPIDITY

Dearest, forgive that with my clumsy touch
    I broke and bruised your rose.
    I hardly could suppose
It were a thing so fragile that my clutch
      Could kill it, thus.

It stood so proudly up upon its stem,
    I knew no thought of fear,
    And coming very near
Fell, overbalanced, to your garment's hem,
      Tearing it down.

Now, stooping, I upgather, one by one,
    The crimson petals, all
    Outspread about my fall.
They hold their fragrance still, a blood-red cone
      Of memory.

And with my words I carve a little jar
    To keep their scented dust,
    Which, opening, you must
Breathe to your soul, and, breathing, know me far
      More grieved than you.

IRONY

An arid daylight shines along the beach
    Dried to a grey monotony of tone,
    And stranded jelly-fish melt soft upon
The sun-baked pebbles, far beyond their reach
Sparkles a wet, reviving sea. Here bleach
    The skeletons of fishes, every bone
    Polished and stark, like traceries of stone,
The joints and knuckles hardened each to each.
    And they are dead while waiting for the sea,
    The moon-pursuing sea, to come again.
Their hearts are blown away on the hot breeze.
    Only the shells and stones can wait to be
    Washed bright. For living things, who suffer pain,
May not endure till time can bring them ease.

HAPPINESS

Happiness, to some, elation;
Is, to others, mere stagnation.
Days of passive somnolence,
At its wildest, indolence.
Hours of empty quietness,
No delight, and no distress.

Happiness to me is wine,
Effervescent, superfine.
Full of tang and fiery pleasure,
Far too hot to leave me leisure
For a single thought beyond it.
Drunk! Forgetful! This the bond: it
Means to give one's soul to gain
Life's quintessence. Even pain
Pricks to livelier living, then
Wakes the nerves to laugh again,
Rapture's self is three parts sorrow.
Although we must die tomorrow,
Losing every thought but this;
Torn, triumphant, drowned in bliss.

Happiness: We rarely feel it.
I would buy it, beg it, steal it,
Pay in coins of dripping blood
For this one transcendent good.

The Last Quarter of the Moon

How long shall I tarnish the mirror of life,
A spatter of rust on its polished steel!
    The seasons reel
    Like a goaded wheel.
Half-numb, half-maddened, my days are strife.

The night is sliding towards the dawn,
And upturned hills crouch at autumn's knees.
    A torn moon flees
    Through the hemlock trees,
The hours have gnawed it to feed their spawn.

Pursuing and jeering the misshapen thing
A rabble of clouds flares out of the east.
    Like dogs unleashed
    After a beast,
They stream on the sky, an outflung string.

A desolate wind, through the unpeopled dark,
Shakes the bushes and whistles through empty nests,
    And the fierce unrests
    I keep as guests
Crowd my brain with corpses, pallid and stark.

Leave me in peace, O Spectres, who haunt
My labouring mind, I have fought and failed.
    I have not quailed,
    I was all unmailed
And naked I strove, 'tis my only vaunt.

The moon drops into the silver day
As waking out of her swoon she comes.
    I hear the drums
    Of millenniums
Beating the mornings I still must stay.

The years I must watch go in and out,
While I build with water, and dig in air,
    And the trumpets blare
    Hollow despair,
The shuddering trumpets of utter rout.

An atom tossed in a chaos made
Of yeasting worlds, which bubble and foam.
    Whence have I come?
    What would be home?
I hear no answer. I am afraid!

I crave to be lost like a wind-blown flame.
Pushed into nothingness by a breath,
    And quench in a wreath
    Of engulfing death
This fight for a God, or this devil's game.

A TALE OF STARVATION

There once was a man whom the gods didn't love,
    And a disagreeable man was he.
He loathed his neighbours, and his neighbours hated him,
    And he cursed eternally.

He damned the sun, and he damned the stars,
    And he blasted the winds in the sky.
He sent to Hell every green, growing thing,
    And he raved at the birds as they fly.

His oaths were many, and his range was wide,
    He swore in fancy ways;
But his meaning was plain: that no created thing
    Was other than a hurt to his gaze.

He dwelt all alone, underneath a leaning hill,
    And windows toward the hill there were none,
And on the other side they were white-washed thick,
    To keep out every spark of the sun.

When he went to market he walked all the way
    Blaspheming at the path he trod.
He cursed at those he bought of, and swore at those he sold to,
    By all the names he knew of God.

For his heart was soured in his weary old hide,
    And his hopes had curdled in his breast.
His friend had been untrue, and his love had thrown him over
    For the chinking money-bags she liked best.

The rats had devoured the contents of his grain-bin,
    The deer had trampled on his corn,
His brook had shrivelled in a summer drought,
    And his sheep had died unshorn.

His hens wouldn't lay, and his cow broke loose,
    And his old horse perished of a colic.
In the loft his wheat-bags were nibbled into holes
    By little, glutton mice on a frolic.

So he slowly lost all he ever had,
    And the blood in his body dried.
Shrunken and mean he still lived on,
    And cursed that future which had lied.

One day he was digging, a spade or two,
    As his aching back could lift,
When he saw something glisten at the bottom of the trench,
    And to get it out he made great shift.

So he dug, and he delved, with care and pain,
    And the veins in his forehead stood taut.
At the end of an hour, when every bone cracked,
    He gathered up what he had sought.

A dim old vase of crusted glass,
    Prismed while it lay buried deep.
Shifting reds and greens, like a pigeon's neck,
    At the touch of the sun began to leap.

It was dull in the tree-shade, but glowing in the light;
    Flashing like an opal-stone,
Carved into a flagon; and the colours glanced and ran,
    Where at first there had seemed to be none.

It had handles on each side to bear it up,
    And a belly for the gurgling wine.
Its neck was slender, and its mouth was wide,
    And its lip was curled and fine.

The old man saw it in the sun's bright stare
    And the colours started up through the crust,
And he who had cursed at the yellow sun
    Held the flask to it and wiped away the dust.

And he bore the flask to the brightest spot,
    Where the shadow of the hill fell clear;
And he turned the flask, and he looked at the flask,
    And the sun shone without his sneer.

Then he carried it home, and put it on a shelf,
    But it was only grey in the gloom.
So he fetched a pail, and a bit of cloth,
    And he went outside with a broom.

And he washed his windows just to let the sun
    Lie upon his new-found vase;
And when evening came, he moved it down
    And put it on a table near the place

Where a candle fluttered in a draught from the door.
    The old man forgot to swear,
Watching its shadow grown a mammoth size,
    Dancing in the kitchen there.

He forgot to revile the sun next morning
    When he found his vase afire in its light.
And he carried it out of the house that day,
    And kept it close beside him until night.

And so it happened from day to day.
    The old man fed his life
On the beauty of his vase, on its perfect shape.
    And his soul forgot its former strife.

And the village-folk came and begged to see
    The flagon which was dug the ground.
And the old man never thought of an oath, in his joy
    At showing what he had found.

One day the master of the village school
    Passed him as he stooped at toil,
Hoeing for a bean-row, and at his side
    Was the vase, on the turned-up soil.

"My friend," said the schoolmaster, pompous and kind,
    "That's a valuable thing you have there,
But it might get broken out of doors,
    It should meet with the utmost care.

What are you doing with it out here?"
    "Why, Sir," said the poor old man,
"I like to have it about, do you see?
    To be with it all I can."

"You will smash it," said the schoolmaster, sternly right,
    "Mark my words and see!"
And he walked away, while the old man looked
    At his treasure despondingly.

Then he smiled to himself, for it was his!
    He had toiled for it, and now he cared.
Yes! loved its shape, and its subtle, swift hues,
    Which his own hard work had bared.

He would carry it round with him everywhere,
    As it gave him joy to do.
A fragile vase should not stand in a bean-row!
    Who would dare to say so? Who?

Then his heart was rested, and his fears gave way,
    And he bent to his hoe again. . .
A clod rolled down, and his foot slipped back,
    And he lurched with a cry of pain.

For the blade of the hoe crashed into glass,
    And the vase fell to iridescent sherds.
The old man's body heaved with slow, dry sobs.
    He did not curse, he had no words.

He gathered the fragments, one by one,
    And his fingers were cut and torn.
Then he made a hole in the very place
    Whence the beautiful vase had been borne.

He covered the hole, and he patted it down,
    Then he hobbled to his house and shut the door.
He tore up his coat and nailed it at the windows
    That no beam of light should cross the floor.

He sat down in front of the empty hearth,
    And he neither ate nor drank.
In three days they found him, dead and cold,
    And they said: "What a queer old crank!"

The Foreigner

Have at you, you Devils!
　My back's to this tree,
For you're nothing so nice
　That the hind-side of me
Would escape your assault.
　Come on now, all three!

Here's a dandified gentleman,
　Rapier at point,
And a wrist which whirls round
　Like a circular joint.
A spatter of blood, man!
　That's just to anoint

And make supple your limbs.
　'Tis a pity the silk
Of your waistcoat is stained.
　Why! Your heart's full of milk,
And so full, it spills over!
　I'm not of your ilk.

You said so, and laughed
　At my old-fashioned hose,
At the cut of my hair,
　At the length of my nose.
To carve it to pattern
　I think you propose.

Your pardon, young Sir,
　But my nose and my sword
Are proving themselves
　In quite perfect accord.
I grieve to have spotted
　Your shirt. On my word!

And hullo! You Bully!
    That blade's not a stick
To slash right and left,
    And my skull is too thick
To be cleft with such cuffs
    Of a sword. Now a lick

Down the side of your face.
    What a pretty, red line!
Tell the taverns that scar
    Was an honour. Don't whine
That a stranger has marked you.
    *   *   *   *   *
    The tree's there, You Swine!

Did you think to get in
    At the back, while your friends
Made a little diversion
    In front? So it ends,
With your sword clattering down
    On the ground. 'Tis amends

I make for your courteous
    Reception of me,
A foreigner, landed
    From over the sea.
Your welcome was fervent
    I think you'll agree.

My shoes are not buckled
    With gold, nor my hair
Oiled and scented, my jacket's
    Not satin, I wear
Corded breeches, wide hats,
    And I make people stare!

So I do, but my heart
    Is the heart of a man,

And my thoughts cannot twirl
    In the limited span
'Twixt my head and my heels,
    As some other men's can.

I have business more strange
    Than the shape of my boots,
And my interests range
    From the sky, to the roots
Of this dung-hill you live in,
    You half-rotted shoots

Of a mouldering tree!
    Here's at you, once more.
You Apes! You Jack-fools!
    You can show me the door,
And jeer at my ways,
    But you're pinked to the core.

And before I have done,
    I will prick my name in
With the front of my steel,
    And your lily-white skin
Shall be printed with me.
    For I've come here to win!

ABSENCE

My cup is empty tonight,
Cold and dry are its sides,
Chilled by the wind from the open window.
Empty and void, it sparkles white in the moonlight.
The room is filled with the strange scent
Of wistaria blossoms.
They sway in the moon's radiance
And tap against the wall.
But the cup of my heart is still,
And cold, and empty.

When you come, it brims
Red and trembling with blood,
Heart's blood for your drinking;
To fill your mouth with love
And the bitter-sweet taste of a soul.

A Gift

See! I give myself to you, Beloved!
My words are little jars
For you to take and put upon a shelf.
Their shapes are quaint and beautiful,
And they have many pleasant colours and lustres
To recommend them.
Also the scent from them fills the room
With sweetness of flowers and crushed grasses.

When I shall have given you the last one,
You will have the whole of me,
But I shall be dead.

The Bungler

You glow in my heart
Like the flames of uncounted candles.
But when I go to warm my hands,
My clumsiness overturns the light,
And then I stumble
Against the tables and chairs.

Fool's Money Bags

Outside the long window,
With his head on the stone sill,
The dog is lying,
Gazing at his Beloved.
His eyes are wet and urgent,
And his body is taut and shaking.
It is cold on the terrace;
A pale wind licks along the stone slabs,
But the dog gazes through the glass
And is content.

The Beloved is writing a letter.
Occasionally she speaks to the dog,
But she is thinking of her writing.
Does she, too, give her devotion to one
Not worthy?

AMY LOWELL

MISCAST I

I have whetted my brain until it is like a Damascus blade,
So keen that it nicks off the floating fringes of passers-by,
So sharp that the air would turn its edge
Were it to be twisted in flight.
Licking passions have bitten their arabesques into it,
And the mark of them lies, in and out,
Worm-like,
With the beauty of corroded copper patterning white steel.
My brain is curved like a scimitar,
And sighs at its cutting
Like a sickle mowing grass.

But of what use is all this to me!
I, who am set to crack stones
In a country lane!

Miscast II

My heart is like a cleft pomegranate
Bleeding crimson seeds
And dripping them on the ground.
My heart gapes because it is ripe and over-full,
And its seeds are bursting from it.

But how is this other than a torment to me!
I, who am shut up, with broken crockery,
In a dark closet!

ANTICIPATION

I have been temperate always,
But I am like to be very drunk
With your coming.
There have been times
I feared to walk down the street
Lest I should reel with the wine of you,
And jerk against my neighbours
As they go by.
I am parched now, and my tongue is horrible in my mouth,
But my brain is noisy
With the clash and gurgle of filling wine-cups.

Vintage

I will mix me a drink of stars,—
Large stars with polychrome needles,
Small stars jetting maroon and crimson,
Cool, quiet, green stars.
I will tear them out of the sky,
And squeeze them over an old silver cup,
And I will pour the cold scorn of my Beloved into it,
So that my drink shall be bubbled with ice.

It will lap and scratch
As I swallow it down;
And I shall feel it as a serpent of fire,
Coiling and twisting in my belly.
His snortings will rise to my head,
And I shall be hot, and laugh,
Forgetting that I have ever known a woman.

THE TREE OF SCARLET BERRIES

The rain gullies the garden paths
And tinkles on the broad sides of grass blades.
A tree, at the end of my arm, is hazy with mist.
Even so, I can see that it has red berries,
A scarlet fruit,
Filmed over with moisture.
It seems as though the rain,
Dripping from it,
Should be tinged with colour.
I desire the berries,
But, in the mist, I only scratch my hand on the thorns.
Probably, too, they are bitter.

Obligation

Hold your apron wide
That I may pour my gifts into it,
So that scarcely shall your two arms hinder them
From falling to the ground.

I would pour them upon you
And cover you,
For greatly do I feel this need
Of giving you something,
Even these poor things.

Dearest of my Heart!

THE TAXI

When I go away from you
The world beats dead
Like a slackened drum.
I call out for you against the jutted stars
And shout into the ridges of the wind.
Streets coming fast,
One after the other,
Wedge you away from me,
And the lamps of the city prick my eyes
So that I can no longer see your face.
Why should I leave you,
To wound myself upon the sharp edges of the night?

The Giver of Stars

Hold your soul open for my welcoming.
Let the quiet of your spirit bathe me
With its clear and rippled coolness,
That, loose-limbed and weary, I find rest,
Outstretched upon your peace, as on a bed of ivory.

Let the flickering flame of your soul play all about me,
That into my limbs may come the keenness of fire,
The life and joy of tongues of flame,
And, going out from you, tightly strung and in tune,
I may rouse the blear-eyed world,
And pour into it the beauty which you have begotten.

AMY LOWELL

The Temple

Between us leapt a gold and scarlet flame.
    Into the hollow of the cupped, arched blue
    Of Heaven it rose. Its flickering tongues up-drew
And vanished in the sunshine. How it came
We guessed not, nor what thing could be its name.
    From each to each had sprung those sparks which flew
    Together into fire. But we knew
The winds would slap and quench it in their game.
    And so we graved and fashioned marble blocks
To treasure it, and placed them round about.
With pillared porticos we wreathed the whole,
    And roofed it with bright bronze. Behind carved locks
Flowered the tall and sheltered flame. Without,
The baffled winds thrust at a column's bole.

Epitaph of a Young Poet Who
Died Before Having Achieved Success

Beneath this sod lie the remains
Of one who died of growing pains.

In Answer to a Request

You ask me for a sonnet. Ah, my Dear,
    Can clocks tick back to yesterday at noon?
    Can cracked and fallen leaves recall last June
And leap up on the boughs, now stiff and sere?
For your sake, I would go and seek the year,
    Faded beyond the purple ranks of dune,
    Blown sands of drifted hours, which the moon
Streaks with a ghostly finger, and her sneer
    Pulls at my lengthening shadow. Yes, 'tis that!
    My shadow stretches forward, and the ground
Is dark in front because the light's behind.
    It is grotesque, with such a funny hat,
    In watching it and walking I have found
More than enough to occupy my mind.

I cannot turn, the light would make me blind.

POPPY SEED

The Great Adventure of Max Breuck

1

A yellow band of light upon the street
Pours from an open door, and makes a wide
Pathway of bright gold across a sheet
Of calm and liquid moonshine. From inside
Come shouts and streams of laughter, and a snatch
Of song, soon drowned and lost again in mirth,
The clip of tankards on a table top,
And stir of booted heels. Against the patch
Of candle-light a shadow falls, its girth
Proclaims the host himself, and master of his shop.

2

This is the tavern of one Hilverdink,
Jan Hilverdink, whose wines are much esteemed.
Within his cellar men can have to drink
The rarest cordials old monks ever schemed
To coax from pulpy grapes, and with nice art
Improve and spice their virgin juiciness.
Here froths the amber beer of many a brew,
Crowning each pewter tankard with as smart
A cap as ever in his wantonness
Winter set glittering on top of an old yew.

3

Tall candles stand upon the table, where
Are twisted glasses, ruby-sparked with wine,
Clarets and ports. Those topaz bumpers were
Drained from slim, long-necked bottles of the Rhine.
The centre of the board is piled with pipes,
Slender and clean, the still unbaptized clay
Awaits its burning fate. Behind, the vault
Stretches from dim to dark, a groping way

Bordered by casks and puncheons, whose brass stripes
And bands gleam dully still, beyond the gay tumult.

4

"For good old Master Hilverdink, a toast!"
Clamoured a youth with tassels on his boots.
"Bring out your oldest brandy for a boast,
From that small barrel in the very roots
Of your deep cellar, man. Why here is Max!
Ho! Welcome, Max, you're scarcely here in time.
We want to drink to old Jan's luck, and smoke
His best tobacco for a grand climax.
Here, Jan, a paper, fragrant as crushed thyme,
We'll have the best to wish you luck, or may we choke!"

5

Max Breuck unclasped his broadcloth cloak, and sat.
"Well thought of, Franz; here's luck to Mynheer Jan."
The host set down a jar; then to a vat
Lost in the distance of his cellar, ran.
Max took a pipe as graceful as the stem
Of some long tulip, crammed it full, and drew
The pungent smoke deep to his grateful lung.
It curled all blue throughout the cave and flew
Into the silver night. At once there flung
Into the crowded shop a boy, who cried to them:

6

"Oh, sirs, is there some learned lawyer here,
Some advocate, or all-wise counsellor?
My master sent me to inquire where
Such men do mostly be, but every door
Was shut and barred, for late has grown the hour.
I pray you tell me where I may now find
One versed in law, the matter will not wait."
"I am a lawyer, boy," said Max, "my mind

Is not locked to my business, though 'tis late.
I shall be glad to serve what way is in my power.

7

Then once more, cloaked and ready, he set out,
Tripping the footsteps of the eager boy
Along the dappled cobbles, while the rout
Within the tavern jeered at his employ.
Through new-burst elm leaves filtered the white moon,
Who peered and splashed between the twinkling boughs,
Flooded the open spaces, and took flight
Before tall, serried houses in platoon,
Guarded by shadows. Past the Custom House
They took their hurried way in the Spring-scented night.

8

Before a door which fronted a canal
The boy halted. A dim tree-shaded spot.
The water lapped the stones in musical
And rhythmic tappings, and a galliot
Slumbered at anchor with no light aboard.
The boy knocked twice, and steps approached. A flame
Winked through the keyhole, then a key was turned,
And through the open door Max went toward
Another door, whence sound of voices came.
He entered a large room where candelabra burned.

9

An aged man in quilted dressing gown
Rose up to greet him. "Sir," said Max, "you sent
Your messenger to seek throughout the town
A lawyer. I have small accomplishment,
But I am at your service, and my name
Is Max Breuck, Counsellor, at your command."
"Mynheer," replied the aged man, "obliged
Am I, and count myself much privileged.

I am Cornelius Kurler, and my fame
Is better known on distant oceans than on land.

10

My ship has tasted water in strange seas,
And bartered goods at still uncharted isles.
She's oft coquetted with a tropic breeze,
And sheered off hurricanes with jaunty smiles."
"Tush, Kurler," here broke in the other man,
"Enough of poetry, draw the deed and sign."
The old man seemed to wizen at the voice,
"My good friend, Grootver,—" he at once began.
"No introductions, let us have some wine,
And business, now that you at last have made your choice."

11

A harsh and disagreeable man he proved to be,
This Grootver, with no single kindly thought.
Kurler explained, his old hands nervously
Twisting his beard. His vessel he had bought
From Grootver. He had thought to soon repay
The ducats borrowed, but an adverse wind
Had so delayed him that his cargo brought
But half its proper price, the very day
He came to port he stepped ashore to find
The market glutted and his counted profits naught.

12

Little by little Max made out the way
That Grootver pressed that poor harassed old man.
His money he must have, too long delay
Had turned the usurer to a ruffian.
"But let me take my ship, with many bales
Of cotton stuffs dyed crimson, green, and blue,
Cunningly patterned, made to suit the taste
Of mandarin's ladies; when my battered sails

Open for home, such stores will I bring you
That all your former ventures will be counted waste.

13

Such light and foamy silks, like crinkled cream,
And indigo more blue than sun-whipped seas,
Spices and fragrant trees, a massive beam
Of sandalwood, and pungent China teas,
Tobacco, coffee!" Grootver only laughed.
Max heard it all, and worse than all he heard
The deed to which the sailor gave his word.
He shivered, 'twas as if the villain gaffed
The old man with a boat-hook; bleeding, spent,
He begged for life nor knew at all the road he went.

14

For Kurler had a daughter, young and gay,
Carefully reared and shielded, rarely seen.
But on one black and most unfriendly day
Grootver had caught her as she passed between
The kitchen and the garden. She had run
In fear of him, his evil leering eye,
And when he came she, bolted in her room,
Refused to show, though gave no reason why.
The spinning of her future had begun,
On quiet nights she heard the whirring of her doom.

15

Max mended an old goosequill by the fire,
Loathing his work, but seeing no thing to do.
He felt his hands were building up the pyre
To burn two souls, and seized with vertigo
He staggered to his chair. Before him lay
White paper still unspotted by a crime.
"Now, young man, write," said Grootver in his ear.
"'If in two years my vessel should yet stay

Of this most sparkling daytime! The crowd swells,
Laughing and pushing toward the quays in friendly strife.

22

The "Horn of Fortune" sails away today.
At highest tide she lets her anchor go,
And starts for China. Saucy popinjay!
Giddy in freshest paint she curtseys low,
And beckons to her boats to let her start.
Blue is the ocean, with a flashing breeze.
The shining waves are quick to take her part.
They push and spatter her. Her sails are loose,
Her tackles hanging, waiting men to seize
And haul them taut, with chanty-singing, as they choose.

23

At the great wharf's edge Mynheer Kurler stands,
And by his side, his daughter, young Christine.
Max Breuck is there, his hat held in his hands,
Bowing before them both. The brigantine
Bounces impatient at the long delay,
Curvets and jumps, a cable's length from shore.
A heavy galliot unloads on the walls
Round, yellow cheeses, like gold cannon balls
Stacked on the stones in pyramids. Once more
Kurler has kissed Christine, and now he is away.

24

Christine stood rigid like a frozen stone,
Her hands wrung pale in effort at control.
Max moved aside and let her be alone,
For grief exacts each penny of its toll.
The dancing boat tossed on the glinting sea.
A sun-path swallowed it in flaming light,
Then, shrunk a cockleshell, it came again
Upon the other side. Now on the lee

It took the "Horn of Fortune." Straining sight
Could see it hauled aboard, men pulling on the crane.

25

Then up above the eager brigantine,
Along her slender masts, the sails took flight,
Were sheeted home, and ropes were coiled. The shine
Of the wet anchor, when its heavy weight
Rose splashing to the deck. These things they saw,
Christine and Max, upon the crowded quay.
They saw the sails grow white, then blue in shade,
The ship had turned, caught in a windy flaw
She glided imperceptibly away,
Drew farther off and in the bright sky seemed to fade.

26

Home, through the emptying streets, Max took Christine,
Who would have hid her sorrow from his gaze.
Before the iron gateway, clasped between
Each garden wall, he stopped. She, in amaze,
Asked, "Do you enter not then, Mynheer Breuck?
My father told me of your courtesy.
Since I am now your charge, 'tis meet for me
To show such hospitality as maiden may,
Without disdaining rules must not be broke.
Katrina will have coffee, and she bakes today."

27

She straight unhasped the tall, beflowered gate.
Curled into tendrils, twisted into cones
Of leaves and roses, iron infoliate,
It guards the pleasance, and its stiffened bones
Are budded with much peering at the rows,
And beds, and arbours, which it keeps inside.
Max started at the beauty, at the glare
Of tints. At either end was set a wide

Path strewn with fine, red gravel, and such shows
Of tulips in their splendour flaunted everywhere!

28

From side to side, midway each path, there ran
A longer one which cut the space in two.
And, like a tunnel some magician
Has wrought in twinkling green, an alley grew,
Pleached thick and walled with apple trees; their flowers
Incensed the garden, and when Autumn came
The plump and heavy apples crowding stood
And tapped against the arbour. Then the dame
Katrina shook them down, in pelting showers
They plunged to earth, and died transformed to sugared food.

29

Against the high, encircling walls were grapes,
Nailed close to feel the baking of the sun
From glowing bricks. Their microscopic shapes
Half hidden by serrated leaves. And one
Old cherry tossed its branches near the door.
Bordered along the wall, in beds between,
Flickering, streaming, nodding in the air,
The pride of all the garden, there were more
Tulips than Max had ever dreamed or seen.
They jostled, mobbed, and danced. Max stood at helpless stare.

30

"Within the arbour, Mynheer Breuck, I'll bring
Coffee and cakes, a pipe, and Father's best
Tobacco, brought from countries harbouring
Dawn's earliest footstep. Wait." With girlish zest
To please her guest she flew. A moment more
She came again, with her old nurse behind.
Then, sitting on the bench and knitting fast,
She talked as someone with a noble store

Of hidden fancies, blown upon the wind,
Eager to flutter forth and leave their silent past.

31

The little apple leaves above their heads
Let fall a quivering sunshine. Quiet, cool,
In blossomed boughs they sat. Beyond, the beds
Of tulips blazed, a proper vestibule
And antechamber to the rainbow. Dyes
Of prismed richness: Carmine. Madder. Blues
Tinging dark browns to purple. Silvers flushed
To amethyst and tinct with gold. Round eyes
Of scarlet, spotting tender saffron hues.
Violets sunk to blacks, and reds in orange crushed.

32

Of every pattern and in every shade.
Nacreous, iridescent, mottled, checked.
Some purest sulphur-yellow, others made
An ivory-white with disks of copper flecked.
Sprinkled and striped, tasselled, or keenest edged.
Striated, powdered, freckled, long or short.
They bloomed, and seemed strange wonder-moths new-fledged,
Born of the spectrum wedded to a flame.
The shade within the arbour made a port
To o'ertaxed eyes, its still, green twilight rest became.

33

Her knitting-needles clicked and Christine talked,
This child matured to woman unaware,
The first time left alone. Now dreams once balked
Found utterance. Max thought her very fair.
Beneath her cap her ornaments shone gold,
And purest gold they were. Kurler was rich
And heedful. Her old maiden aunt had died
Whose darling care she was. Now, growing bold,

She asked, had Max a sister? Dropped a stitch
At her own candour. Then she paused and softly sighed.

34

Two years was long! She loved her father well,
But fears she had not. He had always been
Just sailed or sailing. And she must not dwell
On sad thoughts, he had told her so, and seen
Her smile at parting. But she sighed once more.
Two years was long; 'twas not one hour yet!
Mynheer Grootver she would not see at all.
Yes, yes, she knew, but ere the date so set,
The "Horn of Fortune" would be at the wall.
When Max had bid farewell, she watched him from the door.

35

The next day, and the next, Max went to ask
The health of Jufvrouw Kurler, and the news:
Another tulip blown, or the great task
Of gathering petals which the high wind strews;
The polishing of floors, the pictured tiles
Well scrubbed, and oaken chairs most deftly oiled.
Such things were Christine's world, and his was she
Winter drew near, his sun was in her smiles.
Another Spring, and at his law he toiled,
Unspoken hope counselled a wise efficiency.

36

Max Breuck was honour's soul, he knew himself
The guardian of this girl; no more, no less.
As one in charge of guineas on a shelf
Loose in a china teapot, may confess
His need, but may not borrow till his friend
Comes back to give. So Max, in honour, said
No word of love or marriage; but the days
He clipped off on his almanac. The end

Must come! The second year, with feet of lead,
Lagged slowly by till Spring had plumped the willow sprays.

37

Two years had made Christine a woman grown,
With dignity and gently certain pride.
But all her childhood fancies had not flown,
Her thoughts in lovely dreamings seemed to glide.
Max was her trusted friend, did she confess
A closer happiness? Max could not tell.
Two years were over and his life he found
Sphered and complete. In restless eagerness
He waited for the "Horn of Fortune." Well
Had he his promise kept, abating not one pound.

38

Spring slipped away to Summer. Still no glass
Sighted the brigantine. Then Grootver came
Demanding Jufvrouw Kurler. His trespass
Was justified, for he had won the game.
Christine begged time, more time! Midsummer went,
And Grootver waxed impatient. Still the ship
Tarried. Christine, betrayed and weary, sank
To dreadful terrors. One day, crazed, she sent
For Max. "Come quickly," said her note, "I skip
The worst distress until we meet. The world is blank."

39

Through the long sunshine of late afternoon
Max went to her. In the pleached alley, lost
In bitter reverie, he found her soon.
And sitting down beside her, at the cost
Of all his secret, "Dear," said he, "what thing
So suddenly has happened?" Then, in tears,
She told that Grootver, on the following morn,
Would come to marry her, and shuddering:

"I will die rather, death has lesser fears."
Max felt the shackles drop from the oath which he had sworn.

40

"My Dearest One, the hid joy of my heart!
I love you, oh! you must indeed have known.
In strictest honour I have played my part;
But all this misery has overthrown
My scruples. If you love me, marry me
Before the sun has dipped behind those trees.
You cannot be wed twice, and Grootver, foiled,
Can eat his anger. My care it shall be
To pay your father's debt, by such degrees
As I can compass, and for years I've greatly toiled.

41

This is not haste, Christine, for long I've known
My love, and silence forced upon my lips.
I worship you with all the strength I've shown
In keeping faith." With pleading finger tips
He touched her arm. "Christine! Beloved! Think.
Let us not tempt the future. Dearest, speak,
I love you. Do my words fall too swift now?
They've been in leash so long upon the brink."
She sat quite still, her body loose and weak.
Then into him she melted, all her soul at flow.

42

And they were married ere the westering sun
Had disappeared behind the garden trees.
The evening poured on them its benison,
And flower-scents, that only night-time frees,
Rose up around them from the beamy ground,
Silvered and shadowed by a tranquil moon.
Within the arbour, long they lay embraced,
In such enraptured sweetness as they found

Close-partnered each to each, and thinking soon
To be enwoven, long ere night to morning faced.

43

At last Max spoke, "Dear Heart, this night is ours,
To watch it pale, together, into dawn,
Pressing our souls apart like opening flowers
Until our lives, through quivering bodies drawn,
Are mingled and confounded. Then, far spent,
Our eyes will close to undisturbed rest.
For that desired thing I leave you now.
To pinnacle this day's accomplishment,
By telling Grootver that a bootless quest
Is his, and that his schemes have met a knock-down blow."

44

But Christine clung to him with sobbing cries,
Pleading for love's sake that he leave her not.
And wound her arms about his knees and thighs
As he stood over her. With dread, begot
Of Grootver's name, and silence, and the night,
She shook and trembled. Words in moaning plaint
Wooed him to stay. She feared, she knew not why,
Yet greatly feared. She seemed some anguished saint
Martyred by visions. Max Breuck soothed her fright
With wisdom, then stepped out under the cooling sky.

45

But at the gate once more she held him close
And quenched her heart again upon his lips.
"My Sweetheart, why this terror? I propose
But to be gone one hour! Evening slips
Away, this errand must be done." "Max! Max!
First goes my father, if I lose you now!"
She grasped him as in panic lest she drown.
Softly he laughed, "One hour through the town

By moonlight! That's no place for foul attacks.
Dearest, be comforted, and clear that troubled brow.

46

One hour, Dear, and then, no more alone.
We front another day as man and wife.
I shall be back almost before I'm gone,
And midnight shall anoint and crown our life."
Then through the gate he passed. Along the street
She watched his buttons gleaming in the moon.
He stopped to wave and turned the garden wall.
Straight she sank down upon a mossy seat.
Her senses, mist-encircled by a swoon,
Swayed to unconsciousness beneath its wreathing pall.

47

Briskly Max walked beside the still canal.
His step was firm with purpose. Not a jot
He feared this meeting, nor the rancorous gall
Grootver would spit on him who marred his plot.
He dreaded no man, since he could protect
Christine. His wife! He stopped and laughed aloud.
His starved life had not fitted him for joy.
It strained him to the utmost to reject
Even this hour with her. His heart beat loud.
"Damn Grootver, who can force my time to this employ!"

48

He laughed again. What boyish uncontrol
To be so racked. Then felt his ticking watch.
In half an hour Grootver would know the whole.
And he would be returned, lifting the latch
Of his own gate, eager to take Christine
And crush her to his lips. How bear delay?
He broke into a run. In front, a line
Of candle-light banded the cobbled street.

Hilverdink's tavern! Not for many a day
Had he been there to take his old, accustomed seat.

49

"Why, Max! Stop, Max!" And out they came pell-mell,
His old companions. "Max, where have you been?
Not drink with us? Indeed you serve us well!
How many months is it since we have seen
You here? Jan, Jan, you slow, old doddering goat!
Here's Mynheer Breuck come back again at last,
Stir your old bones to welcome him. Fie, Max.
Business! And after hours! Fill your throat;
Here's beer or brandy. Now, boys, hold him fast.
Put down your cane, dear man. What really vicious whacks!"

50

They forced him to a seat, and held him there,
Despite his anger, while the hideous joke
Was tossed from hand to hand. Franz poured with care
A brimming glass of whiskey. "Here, we've broke
Into a virgin barrel for you, drink!
Tut! Tut! Just hear him! Married! Who, and when?
Married, and out on business. Clever Spark!
Which lie's the likeliest? Come, Max, do think."
Swollen with fury, struggling with these men,
Max cursed hilarity which must needs have a mark.

51

Forcing himself to steadiness, he tried
To quell the uproar, told them what he dared
Of his own life and circumstance. Implied
Most urgent matters, time could ill be spared.
In jesting mood his comrades heard his tale,
And scoffed at it. He felt his anger more
Goaded and bursting;—"Cowards! Is no one loth
To mock at duty—" Here they called for ale,

And forced a pipe upon him. With an oath
He shivered it to fragments on the earthen floor.

52

Sobered a little by his violence,
And by the host who begged them to be still,
Nor injure his good name, "Max, no offence,"
They blurted, "you may leave now if you will."
"One moment, Max," said Franz. "We've gone too far.
I ask your pardon for our foolish joke.
It started in a wager ere you came.
The talk somehow had fall'n on drugs, a jar
I brought from China, herbs the natives smoke,
Was with me, and I thought merely to play a game.

53

Its properties are to induce a sleep
Fraught with adventure, and the flight of time
Is inconceivable in swiftness. Deep
Sunken in slumber, imageries sublime
Flatter the senses, or some fearful dream
Holds them enmeshed. Years pass which on the clock
Are but so many seconds. We agreed
That the next man who came should prove the scheme;
And you were he. Jan handed you the crock.
Two whiffs! And then the pipe was broke, and you were freed."

54

"It is a lie, a damned, infernal lie!"
Max Breuck was maddened now. "Another jest
Of your befuddled wits. I know not why
I am to be your butt. At my request
You'll choose among you one who'll answer for
Your most unseasonable mirth. Good-night
And good-by,—gentlemen. You'll hear from me."
But Franz had caught him at the very door,

"It is no lie, Max Breuck, and for your plight
I am to blame. Come back, and we'll talk quietly.

<h2 style="text-align:center">55</h2>

You have no business, that is why we laughed,
Since you had none a few minutes ago.
As to your wedding, naturally we chaffed,
Knowing the length of time it takes to do
A simple thing like that in this slow world.
Indeed, Max, 'twas a dream. Forgive me then.
I'll burn the drug if you prefer." But Breuck
Muttered and stared,—"A lie." And then he hurled,
Distraught, this word at Franz: "Prove it. And when
It's proven, I'll believe. That thing shall be your work.

<h2 style="text-align:center">56</h2>

I'll give you just one week to make your case.
On August thirty-first, eighteen-fourteen,
I shall require your proof." With wondering face
Franz cried, "A week to August, and fourteen
The year! You're mad, 'tis April now.
April, and eighteen-twelve." Max staggered, caught
A chair,—"April two years ago! Indeed,
Or you, or I, are mad. I know not how
Either could blunder so." Hilverdink brought
"The Amsterdam Gazette," and Max was forced to read.

<h2 style="text-align:center">57</h2>

"Eighteen hundred and twelve," in largest print;
And next to it, "April the twenty-first."
The letters smeared and jumbled, but by dint
Of straining every nerve to meet the worst,
He read it, and into his pounding brain
Tumbled a horror. Like a roaring sea
Foreboding shipwreck, came the message plain:
"This is two years ago! What of Christine?"

He fled the cellar, in his agony
Running to outstrip Fate, and save his holy shrine.

58

The darkened buildings echoed to his feet
Clap-clapping on the pavement as he ran.
Across moon-misted squares clamoured his fleet
And terror-winged steps. His heart began
To labour at the speed. And still no sign,
No flutter of a leaf against the sky.
And this should be the garden wall, and round
The corner, the old gate. No even line
Was this! No wall! And then a fearful cry
Shattered the stillness. Two stiff houses filled the ground.

59

Shoulder to shoulder, like dragoons in line,
They stood, and Max knew them to be the ones
To right and left of Kurler's garden. Spine
Rigid next frozen spine. No mellow tones
Of ancient gilded iron, undulate,
Expanding in wide circles and broad curves,
The twisted iron of the garden gate,
Was there. The houses touched and left no space
Between. With glassy eyes and shaking nerves
Max gazed. Then mad with fear, fled still, and left that place.

60

Stumbling and panting, on he ran, and on.
His slobbering lips could only cry, "Christine!
My Dearest Love! My Wife! Where are you gone?
What future is our past? What saturnine,
Sardonic devil's jest has bid us live
Two years together in a puff of smoke?
It was no dream, I swear it! In some star,
Or still imprisoned in Time's egg, you give

Me love. I feel it. Dearest Dear, this stroke
Shall never part us, I will reach to where you are."

61

His burning eyeballs stared into the dark.
The moon had long been set. And still he cried:
"Christine! My Love! Christine!" A sudden spark
Pricked through the gloom, and shortly Max espied
With his uncertain vision, so within
Distracted he could scarcely trust its truth,
A latticed window where a crimson gleam
Spangled the blackness, and hung from a pin,
An iron crane, were three gilt balls. His youth
Had taught their meaning, now they closed upon his dream.

62

Softly he knocked against the casement, wide
It flew, and a cracked voice his business there
Demanded. The door opened, and inside
Max stepped. He saw a candle held in air
Above the head of a gray-bearded Jew.
"Simeon Isaacs, Mynheer, can I serve
You?" "Yes, I think you can. Do you keep arms?
I want a pistol." Quick the old man grew
Livid. "Mynheer, a pistol! Let me swerve
You from your purpose. Life brings often false alarms—"

63

"Peace, good old Isaacs, why should you suppose
My purpose deadly. In good truth I've been
Blest above others. You have many rows
Of pistols it would seem. Here, this shagreen
Case holds one that I fancy. Silvered mounts
Are to my taste. These letters 'C. D. L.'
Its former owner? Dead, you say. Poor Ghost!
'Twill serve my turn though—" Hastily he counts

The florins down upon the table. "Well,
Good-night, and wish me luck for your tomorrow's toast."

64

Into the night again he hurried, now
Pale and in haste; and far beyond the town
He set his goal. And then he wondered how
Poor C. D. L. had come to die. "It's grown
Handy in killing, maybe, this I've bought,
And will work punctually." His sorrow fell
Upon his senses, shutting out all else.
Again he wept, and called, and blindly fought
The heavy miles away. "Christine. I'm well.
I'm coming. My Own Wife!" He lurched with failing pulse.

65

Along the dyke the keen air blew in gusts,
And grasses bent and wailed before the wind.
The Zuider Zee, which croons all night and thrusts
Long stealthy fingers up some way to find
And crumble down the stones, moaned baffled. Here
The wide-armed windmills looked like gallows-trees.
No lights were burning in the distant thorps.
Max laid aside his coat. His mind, half-clear,
Babbled "Christine!" A shot split through the breeze.
The cold stars winked and glittered at his chilling corpse.

Sancta Maria, Succurre Miseris

Dear Virgin Mary, far away,
Look down from Heaven while I pray.
Open your golden casement high,
And lean way out beyond the sky.
I am so little, it may be
A task for you to harken me.

O Lady Mary, I have bought
A candle, as the good priest taught.
I only had one penny, so
Old Goody Jenkins let it go.
It is a little bent, you see.
But Oh, be merciful to me!

I have not anything to give,
Yet I so long for him to live.
A year ago he sailed away
And not a word unto today.
I've strained my eyes from the sea-wall
But never does he come at all.

Other ships have entered port
Their voyages finished, long or short,
And other sailors have received
Their welcomes, while I sat and grieved.
My heart is bursting for his hail,
O Virgin, let me spy his sail.

> *Hull down on the edge of a sun-soaked sea*
> *Sparkle the bellying sails for me.*
> *Taut to the push of a rousing wind*
> *Shaking the sea till it foams behind,*
> *The tightened rigging is shrill with the song:*
> *"We are back again who were gone so long."*

One afternoon I bumped my head.
I sat on a post and wished I were dead
Like father and mother, for no one cared
Whither I went or how I fared.
A man's voice said, "My little lad,
Here's a bit of a toy to make you glad."

Then I opened my eyes and saw him plain,
With his sleeves rolled up, and the dark blue stain
Of tattooed skin, where a flock of quail
Flew up to his shoulder and met the tail
Of a dragon curled, all pink and green,
Which sprawled on his back, when it was seen.

He held out his hand and gave to me
The most marvellous top which could ever be.
It had ivory eyes, and jet-black rings,
And a red stone carved into little wings,
All joined by a twisted golden line,
And set in the brown wood, even and fine.

Forgive me, Lady, I have not brought
My treasure to you as I ought,
But he said to keep it for his sake
And comfort myself with it, and take
Joy in its spinning, and so I do.
It couldn't mean quite the same to you.

Every day I met him there,
Where the fisher-nets dry in the sunny air.
He told me stories of courts and kings,
Of storms at sea, of lots of things.
The top he said was a sort of sign
That something in the big world was mine.

> *Blue and white on a sun-shot ocean.*
> *Against the horizon a glint in motion.*
> *Full in the grasp of a shoving wind,*

Trailing her bubbles of foam behind,
Singing and shouting to port she races,
A flying harp, with her sheets and braces.

O Queen of Heaven, give me heed,
I am in very utmost need.
He loved me, he was all I had,
And when he came it made the sad
Thoughts disappear. This very day
Send his ship home to me I pray.

I'll be a priest, if you want it so,
I'll work till I have enough to go
And study Latin to say the prayers
On the rosary our old priest wears.
I wished to be a sailor too,
But I will give myself to you.

I'll never even spin my top,
But put it away in a box. I'll stop
Whistling the sailor-songs he taught.
I'll save my pennies till I have bought
A silver heart in the market square,
I've seen some beautiful, white ones there.

I'll give up all I want to do
And do whatever you tell me to.
Heavenly Lady, take away
All the games I like to play,
Take my life to fill the score,
Only bring him back once more!

The poplars shiver and turn their leaves,
And the wind through the belfry moans and grieves.
The gray dust whirls in the market square,
And the silver hearts are covered with care
By thick tarpaulins. Once again
The bay is black under heavy rain.

The Queen of Heaven has shut her door.
A little boy weeps and prays no more.

After Hearing a Waltz by Bartók

But why did I kill him? Why? Why?
　　In the small, gilded room, near the stair?
My ears rack and throb with his cry,
　　And his eyes goggle under his hair,
　　As my fingers sink into the fair
White skin of his throat. It was I!

I killed him! My God! Don't you hear?
　　I shook him until his red tongue
Hung flapping out through the black, queer,
　　Swollen lines of his lips. And I clung
　　With my nails drawing blood, while I flung
The loose, heavy body in fear.

Fear lest he should still not be dead.
　　I was drunk with the lust of his life.
The blood-drops oozed slow from his head
　　And dabbled a chair. And our strife
　　Lasted one reeling second, his knife
Lay and winked in the lights overhead.

And the waltz from the ballroom I heard,
　　When I called him a low, sneaking cur.
And the wail of the violins stirred
　　My brute anger with visions of her.
　　As I throttled his windpipe, the purr
Of his breath with the waltz became blurred.

I have ridden ten miles through the dark,
　　With that music, an infernal din,
Pounding rhythmic inside me. Just Hark!
　　One! Two! Three! And my fingers sink in
　　To his flesh when the violins, thin
And straining with passion, grow stark.

One! Two! Three! Oh, the horror of sound!
    While she danced I was crushing his throat.
He had tasted the joy of her, wound
    Round her body, and I heard him gloat
    On the favour. That instant I smote.
One! Two! Three! How the dancers swirl round!

He is here in the room, in my arm,
    His limp body hangs on the spin
Of the waltz we are dancing, a swarm
    Of blood-drops is hemming us in!
    Round and round! One! Two! Three! And his sin
Is red like his tongue lolling warm.

One! Two! Three! And the drums are his knell.
    He is heavy, his feet beat the floor
As I drag him about in the swell
    Of the waltz. With a menacing roar,
    The trumpets crash in through the door.
One! Two! Three! clangs his funeral bell.

One! Two! Three! In the chaos of space
    Rolls the earth to the hideous glee
Of death! And so cramped is this place,
    I stifle and pant. One! Two! Three!
    Round and round! God! 'Tis he throttles me!
He has covered my mouth with his face!

And his blood has dripped into my heart!
    And my heart beats and labours. One! Two!
Three! His dead limbs have coiled every part
    Of my body in tentacles. Through
    My ears the waltz jangles. Like glue
His dead body holds me athwart.

One! Two! Three! Give me air! Oh! My God!
    One! Two! Three! I am drowning in slime!
One! Two! Three! And his corpse, like a clod,
    Beats me into a jelly! The chime,

    AMY LOWELL

One! Two! Three! And his dead legs keep time.
Air! Give me air! Air! My God!

CLEAR, WITH LIGHT, VARIABLE WINDS

The fountain bent and straightened itself
In the night wind,
Blowing like a flower.
It gleamed and glittered,
A tall white lily,
Under the eye of the golden moon.
From a stone seat,
Beneath a blossoming lime,
The man watched it.
And the spray pattered
On the dim grass at his feet.

The fountain tossed its water,
Up and up, like silver marbles.
Is that an arm he sees?
And for one moment
Does he catch the moving curve
Of a thigh?
The fountain gurgled and splashed,
And the man's face was wet.

Is it singing that he hears?
A song of playing at ball?
The moonlight shines on the straight column of water,
And through it he sees a woman,
Tossing the water-balls.
Her breasts point outwards,
And the nipples are like buds of peonies.
Her flanks ripple as she plays,
And the water is not more undulating
Than the lines of her body.

"Come," she sings, "Poet!
Am I not more worth than your day ladies,
 Covered with awkward stuffs,
 Unreal, unbeautiful?

AMY LOWELL

What do you fear in taking me?
Is not the night for poets?
I am your dream,
Recurrent as water,
Gemmed with the moon!"

She steps to the edge of the pool
And the water runs, rustling, down her sides.
She stretches out her arms,
And the fountain streams behind her
Like an opened veil.

     *   *   *   *   *

In the morning the gardeners came to their work.
"There is something in the fountain," said one.
They shuddered as they laid their dead master
On the grass.
"I will close his eyes," said the head gardener,
"It is uncanny to see a dead man staring at the sun."

The Basket

I

THE INKSTAND IS FULL OF ink, and the paper lies white and unspotted, in the round of light thrown by a candle. Puffs of darkness sweep into the corners, and keep rolling through the room behind his chair. The air is silver and pearl, for the night is liquid with moonlight.

See how the roof glitters, like ice!

Over there, a slice of yellow cuts into the silver-blue, and beside it stand two geraniums, purple because the light is silver-blue, tonight.

See! She is coming, the young woman with the bright hair. She swings a basket as she walks, which she places on the sill, between the geranium stalks. He laughs, and crumples his paper as he leans forward to look. "The Basket Filled with Moonlight," what a title for a book!

The bellying clouds swing over the housetops.

He has forgotten the woman in the room with the geraniums. He is beating his brain, and in his eardrums hammers his heavy pulse. She sits on the window-sill, with the basket in her lap. And tap! She cracks a nut. And tap! Another. Tap! Tap! Tap! The shells ricochet upon the roof, and get into the gutters, and bounce over the edge and disappear.

"It is very queer," thinks Peter, "the basket was empty, I'm sure. How could nuts appear from the atmosphere?"

The silver-blue moonlight makes the geraniums purple, and the roof glitters like ice.

II

FIVE O'CLOCK. THE GERANIUMS ARE very gay in their crimson array. The bellying clouds swing over the housetops, and over the roofs goes Peter to pay his morning's work with a holiday.

"Annette, it is I. Have you finished? Can I come?"

Peter jumps through the window.

"Dear, are you alone?"

"Look, Peter, the dome of the tabernacle is done. This gold thread is so very high, I am glad it is morning, a starry sky would have seen me bankrupt. Sit down, now tell me, is your story going well?"

The golden dome glittered in the orange of the setting sun. On the walls, at intervals, hung altar-cloths and chasubles, and copes, and stoles, and coffin palls. All stiff with rich embroidery, and stitched with so much artistry, they seemed like spun and woven gems, or flower-buds new-opened on their stems.

Annette looked at the geraniums, very red against the blue sky.

"No matter how I try, I cannot find any thread of such a red. My bleeding hearts drip stuff muddy in comparison. Heigh-ho! See my little pecking dove? I'm in love with my own temple. Only that halo's wrong. The colour's too strong, or not strong enough. I don't know. My eyes are tired. Oh, Peter, don't be so rough; it is valuable. I won't do any more. I promise. You tyrannise, Dear, that's enough. Now sit down and amuse me while I rest."

The shadows of the geraniums creep over the floor, and begin to climb the opposite wall.

Peter watches her, fluid with fatigue, floating, and drifting, and undulant in the orange glow. His senses flow towards her, where she lies supine and dreaming. Seeming drowned in a golden halo.

The pungent smell of the geraniums is hard to bear.

He pushes against her knees, and brushes his lips across her languid hands. His lips are hot and speechless. He woos her, quivering, and the room is filled with shadows, for the sun has set. But she only understands the ways of a needle through delicate stuffs, and the shock of one colour on another. She does not see that this is the same, and querulously murmurs his name.

"Peter, I don't want it. I am tired."

And he, the undesired, burns and is consumed.

There is a crescent moon on the rim of the sky.

III

"Go home, now, Peter. Tonight is full moon. I must be alone."

"How soon the moon is full again! Annette, let me stay. Indeed, Dear Love, I shall not go away. My God, but you keep me starved! You write

'No Entrance Here', over all the doors. Is it not strange, my Dear, that loving, yet you deny me entrance everywhere. Would marriage strike you blind, or, hating bonds as you do, why should I be denied the rights of loving if I leave you free? You want the whole of me, you pick my brains to rest you, but you give me not one heart-beat. Oh, forgive me, Sweet! I suffer in my loving, and you know it. I cannot feed my life on being a poet. Let me stay."

"As you please, poor Peter, but it will hurt me if you do. It will crush your heart and squeeze the love out."

He answered gruffly, "I know what I'm about."

"Only remember one thing from tonight. My work is taxing and I must have sight! I *must*!"

The clear moon looks in between the geraniums. On the wall, the shadow of the man is divided from the shadow of the woman by a silver thread.

They are eyes, hundreds of eyes, round like marbles! Unwinking, for there are no lids. Blue, black, gray, and hazel, and the irises are cased in the whites, and they glitter and spark under the moon. The basket is heaped with human eyes. She cracks off the whites and throws them away. They ricochet upon the roof, and get into the gutters, and bounce over the edge and disappear. But she is here, quietly sitting on the window-sill, eating human eyes.

The silver-blue moonlight makes the geraniums purple, and the roof shines like ice.

IV

How hot the sheets are! His skin is tormented with pricks, and over him sticks, and never moves, an eye. It lights the sky with blood, and drips blood. And the drops sizzle on his bare skin, and he smells them burning in, and branding his body with the name "Annette."

The blood-red sky is outside his window now. Is it blood or fire? Merciful God! Fire! And his heart wrenches and pounds "Annette!"

The lead of the roof is scorching, he ricochets, gets to the edge, bounces over and disappears.

The bellying clouds are red as they swing over the housetops.

V

THE AIR IS OF SILVER and pearl, for the night is liquid with moonlight. How the ruin glistens, like a palace of ice! Only two black holes swallow the brilliance of the moon. Deflowered windows, sockets without sight.

A man stands before the house. He sees the silver-blue moonlight, and set in it, over his head, staring and flickering, eyes of geranium red.

Annette!

In a Castle

I

OVER THE YAWNING CHIMNEY HANGS the fog. Drip—hiss—drip—hiss—fall the raindrops on the oaken log which burns, and steams, and smokes the ceiling beams. Drip—hiss—the rain never stops.

The wide, state bed shivers beneath its velvet coverlet. Above, dim, in the smoke, a tarnished coronet gleams dully. Overhead hammers and chinks the rain. Fearfully wails the wind down distant corridors, and there comes the swish and sigh of rushes lifted off the floors. The arras blows sidewise out from the wall, and then falls back again.

It is my lady's key, confided with much nice cunning, whisperingly. He enters on a sob of wind, which gutters the candles almost to swaling. The fire flutters and drops. Drip—hiss—the rain never stops. He shuts the door. The rushes fall again to stillness along the floor. Outside, the wind goes wailing.

The velvet coverlet of the wide bed is smooth and cold. Above, in the firelight, winks the coronet of tarnished gold. The knight shivers in his coat of fur, and holds out his hands to the withering flame. She is always the same, a sweet coquette. He will wait for her.

How the log hisses and drips! How warm and satisfying will be her lips!

It is wide and cold, the state bed; but when her head lies under the coronet, and her eyes are full and wet with love, and when she holds out her arms, and the velvet counterpane half slips from her, and alarms her trembling modesty, how eagerly he will leap to cover her, and blot himself beneath the quilt, making her laugh and tremble.

Is it guilt to free a lady from her palsied lord, absent and fighting, terribly abhorred?

He stirs a booted heel and kicks a rolling coal. His spur clinks on the hearth. Overhead, the rain hammers and chinks. She is so pure and whole. Only because he has her soul will she resign herself to him, for where the soul has gone, the body must be given as a sign. He takes her by the divine right of the only lover. He has sworn to fight her lord, and wed her after. Should he be overborne, she will die adoring him, forlorn, shriven by her great love.

Above, the coronet winks in the darkness. Drip—hiss—fall the raindrops. The arras blows out from the wall, and a door bangs in a far-off hall.

The candles swale. In the gale the moat below plunges and spatters. Will the lady lose courage and not come?
The rain claps on a loosened rafter.
Is that laughter?

The room is filled with lisps and whispers. Something mutters. One candle drowns and the other gutters. Is that the rain which pads and patters, is it the wind through the winding entries which chatters?
The state bed is very cold and he is alone. How far from the wall the arras is blown!

Christ's Death! It is no storm which makes these little chuckling sounds. By the Great Wounds of Holy Jesus, it is his dear lady, kissing and clasping someone! Through the sobbing storm he hears her love take form and flutter out in words. They prick into his ears and stun his desire, which lies within him, hard and dead, like frozen fire. And the little noise never stops.
Drip—hiss—the rain drops.

He tears down the arras from before an inner chamber's bolted door.

II

THE STATE BED SHIVERS IN the watery dawn. Drip—hiss—fall the raindrops. For the storm never stops.
On the velvet coverlet lie two bodies, stripped and fair in the cold, grey air. Drip—hiss—fall the blood-drops, for the bleeding never stops. The bodies lie quietly. At each side of the bed, on the floor, is a head. A man's on this side, a woman's on that, and the red blood oozes along the rush mat.

A wisp of paper is twisted carefully into the strands of the dead man's hair. It says, "My Lord: Your wife's paramour has paid with his life for the high favour."

Through the lady's silver fillet is wound another paper. It reads, "Most noble Lord: Your wife's misdeeds are as a double-stranded necklace of beads. But I have engaged that, on your return, she shall welcome you here. She will not spurn your love as before, you have still the best part of her. Her blood was red, her body white, they will both be here for your delight. The soul inside was a lump of dirt, I have rid you of that with a spurt of my sword point. Good luck to your pleasure. She will be quite complaisant, my friend, I wager." The end was a splashed flourish of ink.

Hark! In the passage is heard the clink of armour, the tread of a heavy man. The door bursts open and standing there, his thin hair wavering in the glare of steely daylight, is my Lord of Clair.

Over the yawning chimney hangs the fog. Drip—hiss—drip—hiss—fall the raindrops. Overhead hammers and chinks the rain which never stops.

The velvet coverlet is sodden and wet, yet the roof beams are tight. Overhead, the coronet gleams with its blackened gold, winking and blinking. Among the rushes three corpses are growing cold.

III

In the castle church you may see them stand,
Two sumptuous tombs on either hand
Of the choir, my Lord's and my Lady's, grand
In sculptured filigrees. And where the transepts of the church expand,
A crusader, come from the Holy Land,
Lies with crossed legs and embroidered band.
The page's name became a brand
For shame. He was buried in crawling sand,
After having been burnt by royal command.

The Bell in the convent tower swung.
High overhead the great sun hung,
A navel for the curving sky.
The air was a blue clarity.
      Swallows flew,
      And a cock crew.

The iron clanging sank through the light air,
Rustled over with blowing branches. A flare
Of spotted green, and a snake had gone
Into the bed where the snowdrops shone
      In green new-started,
      Their white bells parted.

Two by two, in a long brown line,
The nuns were walking to breathe the fine
Bright April air. They must go in soon
And work at their tasks all the afternoon.
      But this time is theirs!
      They walk in pairs.

First comes the Abbess, preoccupied
And slow, as a woman often tried,
With her temper in bond. Then the oldest nun.
Then younger and younger, until the last one
      Has a laugh on her lips,
      And fairly skips.

They wind about the gravel walks
And all the long line buzzes and talks.
They step in time to the ringing bell,
With scarcely a shadow. The sun is well
      In the core of a sky
      Domed silverly.

Sister Marguerite said: "The pears will soon bud."
Sister Angelique said she must get her spud
And free the earth round the jasmine roots.
Sister Veronique said: "Oh, look at those shoots!
        There's a crocus up,
        With a purple cup."

But Sister Clotilde said nothing at all,
She looked up and down the old grey wall
To see if a lizard were basking there.
She looked across the garden to where
        A sycamore
        Flanked the garden door.

She was restless, although her little feet danced,
And quite unsatisfied, for it chanced
Her morning's work had hung in her mind
And would not take form. She could not find
        The beautifulness
        For the Virgin's dress.

Should it be of pink, or damasked blue?
Or perhaps lilac with gold shotted through?
Should it be banded with yellow and white
Roses, or sparked like a frosty night?
        Or a crimson sheen
        Over some sort of green?

But Clotilde's eyes saw nothing new
In all the garden, no single hue
So lovely or so marvellous
That its use would not seem impious.
        So on she walked,
        And the others talked.

Sister Elisabeth edged away
From what her companion had to say,
For Sister Marthe saw the world in little,

She weighed every grain and recorded each tittle.
>She did plain stitching
>And worked in the kitchen.

"Sister Radegonde knows the apples won't last,
I told her so this Friday past.
I must speak to her before Compline."
Her words were like dust motes in slanting sunshine.
>The other nun sighed,
>With her pleasure quite dried.

Suddenly Sister Berthe cried out:
"The snowdrops are blooming!" They turned about.
The little white cups bent over the ground,
And in among the light stems wound
>A crested snake,
>With his eyes awake.

His body was green with a metal brightness
Like an emerald set in a kind of whiteness,
And all down his curling length were disks,
Evil vermilion asterisks,
>They paled and flooded
>As wounds fresh-blooded.

His crest was amber glittered with blue,
And opaque so the sun came shining through.
It seemed a crown with fiery points.
When he quivered all down his scaly joints,
>From every slot
>The sparkles shot.

The nuns huddled tightly together, fear
Catching their senses. But Clotilde must peer
More closely at the beautiful snake,
She seemed entranced and eased. Could she make
>Colours so rare,
>The dress were there.

The Abbess shook off her lethargy.
"Sisters, we will walk on," said she.
Sidling away from the snowdrop bed,
The line curved forwards, the Abbess ahead.
> Only Clotilde
> Was the last to yield.

When the recreation hour was done
Each went in to her task. Alone
In the library, with its great north light,
Clotilde wrought at an exquisite
> Wreath of flowers
> For her Book of Hours.

She twined the little crocus blooms
With snowdrops and daffodils, the glooms
Of laurel leaves were interwoven
With Stars-of-Bethlehem, and cloven
> Fritillaries,
> Whose colour varies.

They framed the picture she had made,
Half-delighted and half-afraid.
In a courtyard with a lozenged floor
The Virgin watched, and through the arched door
> The angel came
> Like a springing flame.

His wings were dipped in violet fire,
His limbs were strung to holy desire.
He lowered his head and passed under the arch,
And the air seemed beating a solemn march.
> The Virgin waited
> With eyes dilated.

Her face was quiet and innocent,
And beautiful with her strange assent.
A silver thread about her head

Her halo was poised. But in the stead
    Of her gown, there remained
    The vellum, unstained.

Clotilde painted the flowers patiently,
Lingering over each tint and dye.
She could spend great pains, now she had seen
That curious, unimagined green.
    A colour so strange
    It had seemed to change.

She thought it had altered while she gazed.
At first it had been simple green; then glazed
All over with twisting flames, each spot
A molten colour, trembling and hot,
    And every eye
    Seemed to liquefy.

She had made a plan, and her spirits danced.
After all, she had only glanced
At that wonderful snake, and she must know
Just what hues made the creature throw
    Those splashes and sprays
    Of prismed rays.

When evening prayers were sung and said,
The nuns lit their tapers and went to bed.
And soon in the convent there was no light,
For the moon did not rise until late that night,
    Only the shine
    Of the lamp at the shrine.

Clotilde lay still in her trembling sheets.
Her heart shook her body with its beats.
She could not see till the moon should rise,
So she whispered prayers and kept her eyes
    On the window-square
    Till light should be there.

The faintest shadow of a branch
Fell on the floor. Clotilde, grown staunch
With solemn purpose, softly rose
And fluttered down between the rows
          Of sleeping nuns.
          She almost runs.

She must go out through the little side door
Lest the nuns who were always praying before
The Virgin's altar should hear her pass.
She pushed the bolts, and over the grass
          The red moon's brim
          Mounted its rim.

Her shadow crept up the convent wall
As she swiftly left it, over all
The garden lay the level glow
Of a moon coming up, very big and slow.
          The gravel glistened.
          She stopped and listened.

It was still, and the moonlight was getting clearer.
She laughed a little, but she felt queerer
Than ever before. The snowdrop bed
Was reached and she bent down her head.
          On the striped ground
          The snake was wound.

For a moment Clotilde paused in alarm,
Then she rolled up her sleeve and stretched out her arm.
She thought she heard steps, she must be quick.
She darted her hand out, and seized the thick
          Wriggling slime,
          Only just in time.

The old gardener came muttering down the path,
And his shadow fell like a broad, black swath,
And covered Clotilde and the angry snake.

He bit her, but what difference did that make!
        The Virgin should dress
        In his loveliness.

The gardener was covering his new-set plants
For the night was chilly, and nothing daunts
Your lover of growing things. He spied
Something to do and turned aside,
        And the moonlight streamed
        On Clotilde, and gleamed.

His business finished the gardener rose.
He shook and swore, for the moonlight shows
A girl with a fire-tongued serpent, she
Grasping him, laughing, while quietly
        Her eyes are weeping.
        Is he sleeping?

He thinks it is some holy vision,
Brushes that aside and with decision
Jumps—and hits the snake with his stick,
Crushes his spine, and then with quick,
        Urgent command
        Takes her hand.

The gardener sucks the poison and spits,
Cursing and praying as befits
A poor old man half out of his wits.
"Whatever possessed you, Sister, it's
        Hatched of a devil
        And very evil.

It's one of them horrid basilisks
You read about. They say a man risks
His life to touch it, but I guess I've sucked it
Out by now. Lucky I chucked it
        Away from you.
        I guess you'll do."

"Oh, no, Francois, this beautiful beast
Was sent to me, to me the least
Worthy in all our convent, so I
Could finish my picture of the Most High
        And Holy Queen,
        In her dress of green.

He is dead now, but his colours won't fade
At once, and by noon I shall have made
The Virgin's robe. Oh, Francois, see
How kindly the moon shines down on me!
        I can't die yet,
        For the task was set."

"You won't die now, for I've sucked it away,"
Grumbled old Francois, "so have your play.
If the Virgin is set on snake's colours so strong,—"
"Francois, don't say things like that, it is wrong."
        So Clotilde vented
        Her creed. He repented.

"He can't do no more harm, Sister," said he.
"Paint as much as you like." And gingerly
He picked up the snake with his stick. Clotilde
Thanked him, and begged that he would shield
        Her secret, though itching
        To talk in the kitchen.

The gardener promised, not very pleased,
And Clotilde, with the strain of adventure eased,
Walked quickly home, while the half-high moon
Made her beautiful snake-skin sparkle, and soon
        In her bed she lay
        And waited for day.

At dawn's first saffron-spired warning
Clotilde was up. And all that morning,
Except when she went to the chapel to pray,

She painted, and when the April day
    Was hot with sun,
    Clotilde had done.

Done! She drooped, though her heart beat loud
At the beauty before her, and her spirit bowed
To the Virgin her finely-touched thought had made.
A lady, in excellence arrayed,
    And wonder-souled.
    Christ's Blessed Mould!

From long fasting Clotilde felt weary and faint,
But her eyes were starred like those of a saint
Enmeshed in Heaven's beatitude.
A sudden clamour hurled its rude
    Force to break
    Her vision awake.

The door nearly leapt from its hinges, pushed
By the multitude of nuns. They hushed
When they saw Clotilde, in perfect quiet,
Smiling, a little perplexed at the riot.
    And all the hive
    Buzzed "She's alive!"

Old Francois had told. He had found the strain
Of silence too great, and preferred the pain
Of a conscience outraged. The news had spread,
And all were convinced Clotilde must be dead.
    For Francois, to spite them,
    Had not seen fit to right them.

The Abbess, unwontedly trembling and mild,
Put her arms round Clotilde and wept, "My child,
Has the Holy Mother showed you this grace,
To spare you while you imaged her face?
    How could we have guessed
    Our convent so blessed!

A miracle! But Oh! My Lamb!
To have you die! And I, who am
A hollow, living shell, the grave
Is empty of me. Holy Mary, I crave
      To be taken, Dear Mother,
      Instead of this other."

She dropped on her knees and silently prayed,
With anguished hands and tears delayed
To a painful slowness. The minutes drew
To fractions. Then the west wind blew
      The sound of a bell,
      On a gusty swell.

It came skipping over the slates of the roof,
And the bright bell-notes seemed a reproof
To grief, in the eye of so fair a day.
The Abbess, comforted, ceased to pray.
      And the sun lit the flowers
      In Clotilde's Book of Hours.

It glistened the green of the Virgin's dress
And made the red spots, in a flushed excess,
Pulse and start; and the violet wings
Of the angel were colour which shines and sings.
      The book seemed a choir
      Of rainbow fire.

The Abbess crossed herself, and each nun
Did the same, then one by one,
They filed to the chapel, that incensed prayers
Might plead for the life of this sister of theirs.
      Clotilde, the Inspired!

      She only felt tired.
      *   *   *   *   *
The old chronicles say she did not die
Until heavy with years. And that is why
There hangs in the convent church a basket

                                               AMY LOWELL

Of osiered silver, a holy casket,
        And treasured therein
        A dried snake-skin.

THE EXETER ROAD

Panels of claret and blue which shine
Under the moon like lees of wine.
A coronet done in a golden scroll,
And wheels which blunder and creak as they roll
Through the muddy ruts of a moorland track.
      They daren't look back!

They are whipping and cursing the horses. Lord!
What brutes men are when they think they're scored.
Behind, my bay gelding gallops with me,
In a steaming sweat, it is fine to see
That coach, all claret, and gold, and blue,
      Hop about and slue.

They are scared half out of their wits, poor souls.
For my lord has a casket full of rolls
Of minted sovereigns, and silver bars.
I laugh to think how he'll show his scars
In London tomorrow. He whines with rage
      In his varnished cage.

My lady has shoved her rings over her toes.
'Tis an ancient trick every night-rider knows.
But I shall relieve her of them yet,
When I see she limps in the minuet
I must beg to celebrate this night,
      And the green moonlight.

There's nothing to hurry about, the plain
Is hours long, and the mud's a strain.
My gelding's uncommonly strong in the loins,
In half an hour I'll bag the coins.
'Tis a clear, sweet night on the turn of Spring.
      The chase is the thing!

How the coach flashes and wobbles, the moon
Dripping down so quietly on it. A tune
Is beating out of the curses and screams,
And the cracking all through the painted seams.
Steady, old horse, we'll keep it in sight.
      'Tis a rare fine night!

There's a clump of trees on the dip of the down,
And the sky shimmers where it hangs over the town.
It seems a shame to break the air
In two with this pistol, but I've my share
Of drudgery like other men.
      His hat? Amen!

Hold up, you beast, now what the devil!
Confound this moor for a pockholed, evil,
Rotten marsh. My right leg's snapped.
'Tis a mercy he's rolled, but I'm nicely capped.
A broken-legged man and a broken-legged horse!
      They'll get me, of course.

The cursed coach will reach the town
And they'll all come out, every loafer grown
A lion to handcuff a man that's down.
What's that? Oh, the coachman's bulleted hat!
I'll give it a head to fit it pat.
      Thank you! No cravat.

They handcuffed the body just for style,
And they hung him in chains for the volatile
Wind to scour him flesh from bones.
Way out on the moor you can hear the groans
His gibbet makes when it blows a gale.
      'Tis a common tale.

The Shadow

Paul Jannes was working very late,
For this watch must be done by eight
Tomorrow or the Cardinal
Would certainly be vexed. Of all
His customers the old prelate
Was the most important, for his state
Descended to his watches and rings,
And he gave his mistresses many things
To make them forget his age and smile
When he paid visits, and they could while
The time away with a diamond locket
Exceedingly well. So they picked his pocket,
And he paid in jewels for his slobbering kisses.
This watch was made to buy him blisses
From an Austrian countess on her way
Home, and she meant to start next day.

Paul worked by the pointed, tulip-flame
Of a tallow candle, and became
So absorbed, that his old clock made him wince
Striking the hour a moment since.
Its echo, only half apprehended,
Lingered about the room. He ended
Screwing the little rubies in,
Setting the wheels to lock and spin,
Curling the infinitesimal springs,
Fixing the filigree hands. Chippings
Of precious stones lay strewn about.
The table before him was a rout
Of splashes and sparks of coloured light.
There was yellow gold in sheets, and quite
A heap of emeralds, and steel.
Here was a gem, there was a wheel.
And glasses lay like limpid lakes
Shining and still, and there were flakes

Of silver, and shavings of pearl,
And little wires all awhirl
With the light of the candle. He took the watch
And wound its hands about to match
The time, then glanced up to take the hour
From the hanging clock.

                    Good, Merciful Power!
How came that shadow on the wall,
No woman was in the room! His tall
Chiffonier stood gaunt behind
His chair. His old cloak, rabbit-lined,
Hung from a peg. The door was closed.
Just for a moment he must have dozed.
He looked again, and saw it plain.
The silhouette made a blue-black stain
On the opposite wall, and it never wavered
Even when the candle quavered
Under his panting breath. What made
That beautiful, dreadful thing, that shade
Of something so lovely, so exquisite,
Cast from a substance which the sight
Had not been tutored to perceive?
Paul brushed his eyes across his sleeve.

Clear-cut, the Shadow on the wall
Gleamed black, and never moved at all.

Paul's watches were like amulets,
Wrought into patterns and rosettes;
The cases were all set with stones,
And wreathing lines, and shining zones.
He knew the beauty in a curve,
And the Shadow tortured every nerve
With its perfect rhythm of outline
Cutting the whitewashed wall. So fine
Was the neck he knew he could have spanned
It about with the fingers of one hand.
The chin rose to a mouth he guessed,

But could not see, the lips were pressed
Loosely together, the edges close,
And the proud and delicate line of the nose
Melted into a brow, and there
Broke into undulant waves of hair.
The lady was edged with the stamp of race.
A singular vision in such a place.

He moved the candle to the tall
Chiffonier; the Shadow stayed on the wall.
He threw his cloak upon a chair,
And still the lady's face was there.
From every corner of the room
He saw, in the patch of light, the gloom
That was the lady. Her violet bloom
Was almost brighter than that which came
From his candle's tulip-flame.
He set the filigree hands; he laid
The watch in the case which he had made;
He put on his rabbit cloak, and snuffed
His candle out. The room seemed stuffed
With darkness. Softly he crossed the floor,
And let himself out through the door.

The sun was flashing from every pin
And wheel, when Paul let himself in.
The whitewashed walls were hot with light.
The room was the core of a chrysolite,
Burning and shimmering with fiery might.
The sun was so bright that no shadow could fall
From the furniture upon the wall.
Paul sighed as he looked at the empty space
Where a glare usurped the lady's place.
He settled himself to his work, but his mind
Wandered, and he would wake to find
His hand suspended, his eyes grown dim,

And nothing advanced beyond the rim
Of his dreaming. The Cardinal sent to pay
For his watch, which had purchased so fine a day.
But Paul could hardly touch the gold,
It seemed the price of his Shadow, sold.
With the first twilight he struck a match
And watched the little blue stars hatch
Into an egg of perfect flame.
He lit his candle, and almost in shame
At his eagerness, lifted his eyes.
The Shadow was there, and its precise
Outline etched the cold, white wall.
The young man swore, "By God! You, Paul,
There's something the matter with your brain.
Go home now and sleep off the strain."

The next day was a storm, the rain
Whispered and scratched at the window-pane.
A grey and shadowless morning filled
The little shop. The watches, chilled,
Were dead and sparkless as burnt-out coals.
The gems lay on the table like shoals
Of stranded shells, their colours faded,
Mere heaps of stone, dull and degraded.
Paul's head was heavy, his hands obeyed
No orders, for his fancy strayed.
His work became a simple round
Of watches repaired and watches wound.
The slanting ribbons of the rain
Broke themselves on the window-pane,
But Paul saw the silver lines in vain.
Only when the candle was lit
And on the wall just opposite
He watched again the coming of *it*,
Could he trace a line for the joy of his soul
And over his hands regain control.

Paul lingered late in his shop that night
And the designs which his delight
Sketched on paper seemed to be
A tribute offered wistfully
To the beautiful shadow of her who came
And hovered over his candle flame.
In the morning he selected all
His perfect jacinths. One large opal
Hung like a milky, rainbow moon
In the centre, and blown in loose festoon
The red stones quivered on silver threads
To the outer edge, where a single, fine
Band of mother-of-pearl the line
Completed. On the other side,
The creamy porcelain of the face
Bore diamond hours, and no lace
Of cotton or silk could ever be
Tossed into being more airily
Than the filmy golden hands; the time
Seemed to tick away in rhyme.
When, at dusk, the Shadow grew
Upon the wall, Paul's work was through.
Holding the watch, he spoke to her:
"Lady, Beautiful Shadow, stir
Into one brief sign of being.
Turn your eyes this way, and seeing
This watch, made from those sweet curves
Where your hair from your forehead swerves,
Accept the gift which I have wrought
With your fairness in my thought.
Grant me this, and I shall be
Honoured overwhelmingly."

The Shadow rested black and still,
And the wind sighed over the window-sill.

Paul put the despised watch away
And laid out before him his array

Of stones and metals, and when the morning
Struck the stones to their best adorning,
He chose the brightest, and this new watch
Was so light and thin it seemed to catch
The sunlight's nothingness, and its gleam.
Topazes ran in a foamy stream
Over the cover, the hands were studded
With garnets, and seemed red roses, budded.
The face was of crystal, and engraved
Upon it the figures flashed and waved
With zircons, and beryls, and amethysts.
It took a week to make, and his trysts
At night with the Shadow were his alone.
Paul swore not to speak till his task was done.
The night that the jewel was worthy to give.
Paul watched the long hours of daylight live
To the faintest streak; then lit his light,
And sharp against the wall's pure white
The outline of the Shadow started
Into form. His burning-hearted
Words so long imprisoned swelled
To tumbling speech. Like one compelled,
He told the lady all his love,
And holding out the watch above
His head, he knelt, imploring some
Littlest sign.
              The Shadow was dumb.

Weeks passed, Paul worked in fevered haste,
And everything he made he placed
Before his lady. The Shadow kept
Its perfect passiveness. Paul wept.
He wooed her with the work of his hands,
He waited for those dear commands
She never gave. No word, no motion,
Eased the ache of his devotion.
His days passed in a strain of toil,
His nights burnt up in a seething coil.

Seasons shot by, uncognisant
He worked. The Shadow came to haunt
Even his days. Sometimes quite plain
He saw on the wall the blackberry stain
Of his lady's picture. No sun was bright
Enough to dazzle that from his sight.

There were moments when he groaned to see
His life spilled out so uselessly,
Begging for boons the Shade refused,
His finest workmanship abused,
The iridescent bubbles he blew
Into lovely existence, poor and few
In the shadowed eyes. Then he would curse
Himself and her! The Universe!
And more, the beauty he could not make,
And give her, for her comfort's sake!
He would beat his weary, empty hands
Upon the table, would hold up strands
Of silver and gold, and ask her why
She scorned the best which he could buy.
He would pray as to some high-niched saint,
That she would cure him of the taint
Of failure. He would clutch the wall
With his bleeding fingers, if she should fall
He could catch, and hold her, and make her live!
With sobs he would ask her to forgive
All he had done. And broken, spent,
He would call himself impertinent;
Presumptuous; a tradesman; a nothing; driven
To madness by the sight of Heaven.
At other times he would take the things
He had made, and winding them on strings,
Hang garlands before her, and burn perfumes,
Chanting strangely, while the fumes
Wreathed and blotted the shadow face,
As with a cloudy, nacreous lace.
There were days when he wooed as a lover, sighed

In tenderness, spoke to his bride,
Urged her to patience, said his skill
Should break the spell. A man's sworn will
Could compass life, even that, he knew.
By Christ's Blood! He would prove it true!

The edge of the Shadow never blurred.
The lips of the Shadow never stirred.

He would climb on chairs to reach her lips,
And pat her hair with his finger-tips.
But instead of young, warm flesh returning
His warmth, the wall was cold and burning
Like stinging ice, and his passion, chilled,
Lay in his heart like some dead thing killed
At the moment of birth. Then, deadly sick,
He would lie in a swoon for hours, while thick
Phantasmagoria crowded his brain,
And his body shrieked in the clutch of pain.
The crisis passed, he would wake and smile
With a vacant joy, half-imbecile
And quite confused, not being certain
Why he was suffering; a curtain
Fallen over the tortured mind beguiled
His sorrow. Like a little child
He would play with his watches and gems, with glee
Calling the Shadow to look and see
How the spots on the ceiling danced prettily
When he flashed his stones. "Mother, the green
Has slid so cunningly in between
The blue and the yellow. Oh, please look down!"
Then, with a pitiful, puzzled frown,
He would get up slowly from his play
And walk round the room, feeling his way
From table to chair, from chair to door,
Stepping over the cracks in the floor,
Till reaching the table again, her face
Would bring recollection, and no solace

Could balm his hurt till unconsciousness
Stifled him and his great distress.

One morning he threw the street door wide
On coming in, and his vigorous stride
Made the tools on his table rattle and jump.
In his hands he carried a new-burst clump
Of laurel blossoms, whose smooth-barked stalks
Were pliant with sap. As a husband talks
To the wife he left an hour ago,
Paul spoke to the Shadow. "Dear, you know
Today the calendar calls it Spring,
And I woke this morning gathering
Asphodels, in my dreams, for you.
So I rushed out to see what flowers blew
Their pink-and-purple-scented souls
Across the town-wind's dusty scrolls,
And made the approach to the Market Square
A garden with smells and sunny air.
I feel so well and happy today,
I think I shall take a Holiday.
And tonight we will have a little treat.
I am going to bring you something to eat!"
He looked at the Shadow anxiously.
It was quite grave and silent. He
Shut the outer door and came
And leant against the window-frame.
"Dearest," he said, "we live apart
Although I bear you in my heart.
We look out each from a different world.
At any moment we may be hurled
Asunder. They follow their orbits, we
Obey their laws entirely.
Now you must come, or I go there,
Unless we are willing to live the flare
Of a lighted instant and have it gone."

A bee in the laurels began to drone.
A loosened petal fluttered prone.

"Man grows by eating, if you eat
You will be filled with our life, sweet
Will be our planet in your mouth.
If not, I must parch in death's wide drouth
Until I gain to where you are,
And give you myself in whatever star
May happen. O You Beloved of Me!
Is it not ordered cleverly?"

The Shadow, bloomed like a plum, and clear,
Hung in the sunlight. It did not hear.

Paul slipped away as the dusk began
To dim the little shop. He ran
To the nearest inn, and chose with care
As much as his thin purse could bear.
As rapt-souled monks watch over the baking
Of the sacred wafer, and through the making
Of the holy wine whisper secret prayers
That God will bless this labour of theirs;
So Paul, in a sober ecstasy,
Purchased the best which he could buy.
Returning, he brushed his tools aside,
And laid across the table a wide
Napkin. He put a glass and plate
On either side, in duplicate.
Over the lady's, excellent
With loveliness, the laurels bent.
In the centre the white-flaked pastry stood,
And beside it the wine flask. Red as blood
Was the wine which should bring the lustihood
Of human life to his lady's veins.
When all was ready, all which pertains
To a simple meal was there, with eyes

Lit by the joy of his great emprise,
He reverently bade her come,
And forsake for him her distant home.
He put meat on her plate and filled her glass,
And waited what should come to pass.

The Shadow lay quietly on the wall.
From the street outside came a watchman's call
"A cloudy night. Rain beginning to fall."

And still he waited. The clock's slow tick
Knocked on the silence. Paul turned sick.

He filled his own glass full of wine;
From his pocket he took a paper. The twine
Was knotted, and he searched a knife
From his jumbled tools. The cord of life
Snapped as he cut the little string.
He knew that he must do the thing
He feared. He shook powder into the wine,
And holding it up so the candle's shine
Sparked a ruby through its heart,
He drank it. "Dear, never apart
Again! You have said it was mine to do.
It is done, and I am come to you!"

Paul Jannes let the empty wine-glass fall,
And held out his arms. The insentient wall
Stared down at him with its cold, white glare
Unstained! The Shadow was not there!
Paul clutched and tore at his tightening throat.
He felt the veins in his body bloat,
And the hot blood run like fire and stones
Along the sides of his cracking bones.
But he laughed as he staggered towards the door,
And he laughed aloud as he sank on the floor.

The Coroner took the body away,
And the watches were sold that Saturday.
The Auctioneer said one could seldom buy
Such watches, and the prices were high.

The Forsaken

Holy Mother of God, Merciful Mary. Hear me! I am very weary. I have come from a village miles away, all day I have been coming, and I ache for such far roaming. I cannot walk as light as I used, and my thoughts grow confused. I am heavier than I was. Mary Mother, you know the cause!

Beautiful Holy Lady, take my shame away from me! Let this fear be only seeming, let it be that I am dreaming. For months I have hoped it was so, now I am afraid I know. Lady, why should this be shame, just because I haven't got his name. He loved me, yes, Lady, he did, and he couldn't keep it hid. We meant to marry. Why did he die?

That day when they told me he had gone down in the avalanche, and could not be found until the snow melted in Spring, I did nothing. I could not cry. Why should he die? Why should he die and his child live? His little child alive in me, for my comfort. No, Good God, for my misery! I cannot face the shame, to be a mother, and not married, and the poor child to be reviled for having no father. Merciful Mother, Holy Virgin, take away this sin I did. Let the baby not be. Only take the stigma off of me!

I have told no one but you, Holy Mary. My mother would call me "whore," and spit upon me; the priest would have me repent, and have the rest of my life spent in a convent. I am no whore, no bad woman, he loved me, and we were to be married. I carried him always in my heart, what did it matter if I gave him the least part of me too? You were a virgin, Holy Mother, but you had a son, you know there are times when a woman must give all. There is some call to give and hold back nothing. I swear I obeyed God then, and this child who lives in me is the sign. What am I saying? He is dead, my beautiful, strong man! I shall never feel him caress me again. This is the only baby I shall have. Oh, Holy Virgin, protect my baby! My little, helpless baby!

He will look like his father, and he will be as fast a runner and as good a shot. Not that he shall be no scholar neither. He shall go to school in winter, and learn to read and write, and my father will teach him to carve, so that he can make the little horses, and cows, and chamois, out of white wood. Oh, No! No! No! How can I think such things, I am not good. My father will have nothing to do with my boy, I shall be an outcast thing. Oh, Mother of our Lord God, be merciful, take away my shame! Let my body be as it was before he came. No little baby for me to keep underneath my heart for those long months. To live for and to get comfort from. I cannot go home and tell my mother. She is so hard and righteous. She never loved my father, and we were born for duty, not for love. I cannot face it. Holy Mother, take my baby away! Take away my little baby! I don't want it, I can't bear it!

And I shall have nothing, nothing! Just be known as a good girl. Have other men want to marry me, whom I could not touch, after having known my man. Known the length and breadth of his beautiful white body, and the depth of his love, on the high Summer Alp, with the moon above, and the pine-needles all shiny in the light of it. He is gone, my man, I shall never hear him or feel him again, but I could not touch another. I would rather lie under the snow with my own man in my arms!

So I shall live on and on. Just a good woman. With nothing to warm my heart where he lay, and where he left his baby for me to care for. I shall not be quite human, I think. Merely a stone-dead creature. They will respect me. What do I care for respect! You didn't care for people's tongues when you were carrying our Lord Jesus. God had my man give me my baby, when He knew that He was going to take him away. His lips will comfort me, his hands will soothe me. All day I will work at my lace-making, and all night I will keep him warm by my side and pray the blessed Angels to cover him with their wings. Dear Mother, what is it that sings? I hear voices singing, and lovely silver trumpets through it all. They seem just on the other side of the wall. Let me keep my baby, Holy Mother. He is only a poor lace-maker's baby, with a stain upon him, but give me strength to bring him up to be a man.

LATE SEPTEMBER

Tang of fruitage in the air;
Red boughs bursting everywhere;
Shimmering of seeded grass;
Hooded gentians all a'mass.

Warmth of earth, and cloudless wind
Tearing off the husky rind,
Blowing feathered seeds to fall
By the sun-baked, sheltering wall.

Beech trees in a golden haze;
Hardy sumachs all ablaze,
Glowing through the silver birches.
How that pine tree shouts and lurches!

From the sunny door-jamb high,
Swings the shell of a butterfly.
Scrape of insect violins
Through the stubble shrilly dins.

Every blade's a minaret
Where a small muezzin's set,
Loudly calling us to pray
At the miracle of day.

Then the purple-lidded night
Westering comes, her footsteps light
Guided by the radiant boon
Of a sickle-shaped new moon.

The Pike

In the brown water,
Thick and silver-sheened in the sunshine,
Liquid and cool in the shade of the reeds,
A pike dozed.
Lost among the shadows of stems
He lay unnoticed.
Suddenly he flicked his tail,
And a green-and-copper brightness
Ran under the water.

Out from under the reeds
Came the olive-green light,
And orange flashed up
Through the sun-thickened water.
So the fish passed across the pool,
Green and copper,
A darkness and a gleam,
And the blurred reflections of the willows on the opposite bank
Received it.

The Blue Scarf

Pale, with the blue of high zeniths, shimmered over with silver, brocaded
In smooth, running patterns, a soft stuff, with dark knotted fringes, it lies there,
Warm from a woman's soft shoulders, and my fingers close on it, caressing.
Where is she, the woman who wore it? The scent of her lingers and drugs me!
A languor, fire-shotted, runs through me, and I crush the scarf down on my face,
And gulp in the warmth and the blueness, and my eyes swim in cool-tinted heavens.
Around me are columns of marble, and a diapered, sun-flickered pavement.
Rose-leaves blow and patter against it. Below the stone steps a lute tinkles.
A jar of green jade throws its shadow half over the floor. A big-bellied
Frog hops through the sunlight and plops in the gold-bubbled water of a basin,
Sunk in the black and white marble. The west wind has lifted a scarf
On the seat close beside me, the blue of it is a violent outrage of colour.
She draws it more closely about her, and it ripples beneath her slight stirring.
Her kisses are sharp buds of fire; and I burn back against her, a jewel
Hard and white; a stalked, flaming flower; till I break to a handful of cinders,
And open my eyes to the scarf, shining blue in the afternoon sunshine.

How loud clocks can tick when a room is empty, and one is alone!

WHITE AND GREEN

Hey! My daffodil-crowned,
Slim and without sandals!
As the sudden spurt of flame upon darkness
So my eyeballs are startled with you,
Supple-limbed youth among the fruit-trees,
Light runner through tasselled orchards.
You are an almond flower unsheathed
Leaping and flickering between the budded branches.

Aubade

As I would free the white almond from the green husk
So would I strip your trappings off,
Beloved.
And fingering the smooth and polished kernel
I should see that in my hands glittered a gem beyond counting.

Music

The neighbour sits in his window and plays the flute.
From my bed I can hear him,
And the round notes flutter and tap about the room,
And hit against each other,
Blurring to unexpected chords.
It is very beautiful,
With the little flute-notes all about me,
In the darkness.

In the daytime,
The neighbour eats bread and onions with one hand
And copies music with the other.
He is fat and has a bald head,
So I do not look at him,
But run quickly past his window.
There is always the sky to look at,
Or the water in the well!

But when night comes and he plays his flute,
I think of him as a young man,
With gold seals hanging from his watch,
And a blue coat with silver buttons.
As I lie in my bed
The flute-notes push against my ears and lips,
And I go to sleep, dreaming.

A Lady

You are beautiful and faded
Like an old opera tune
Played upon a harpsichord;
Or like the sun-flooded silks
Of an eighteenth-century boudoir.
In your eyes
Smoulder the fallen roses of out-lived minutes,
And the perfume of your soul
Is vague and suffusing,
With the pungence of sealed spice-jars.
Your half-tones delight me,
And I grow mad with gazing
At your blent colours.

My vigour is a new-minted penny,
Which I cast at your feet.
Gather it up from the dust,
That its sparkle may amuse you.

In a Garden

Gushing from the mouths of stone men
To spread at ease under the sky
In granite-lipped basins,
Where iris dabble their feet
And rustle to a passing wind,
The water fills the garden with its rushing,
In the midst of the quiet of close-clipped lawns.

Damp smell the ferns in tunnels of stone,
Where trickle and plash the fountains,
Marble fountains, yellowed with much water.

Splashing down moss-tarnished steps
It falls, the water;
And the air is throbbing with it.
With its gurgling and running.
With its leaping, and deep, cool murmur.

And I wished for night and you.
I wanted to see you in the swimming-pool,
White and shining in the silver-flecked water.
While the moon rode over the garden,
High in the arch of night,
And the scent of the lilacs was heavy with stillness.

Night, and the water, and you in your whiteness, bathing!

A Tulip Garden

Guarded within the old red wall's embrace,
   Marshalled like soldiers in gay company,
   The tulips stand arrayed. Here infantry
Wheels out into the sunlight. What bold grace
Sets off their tunics, white with crimson lace!
   Here are platoons of gold-frocked cavalry,
   With scarlet sabres tossing in the eye
Of purple batteries, every gun in place.
   Forward they come, with flaunting colours spread,
With torches burning, stepping out in time
   To some quick, unheard march. Our ears are dead,
We cannot catch the tune. In pantomime
   Parades that army. With our utmost powers
   We hear the wind stream through a bed of flowers.

A Note About the Author

Amy Lowell (1874–1925) was an American poet. Born into an elite family of businessmen, politicians, and intellectuals, Lowell was a member of the so-called Boston Brahmin class. She excelled in school from a young age and developed a habit for reading and book collecting. Denied the opportunity to attend college by her family, Lowell traveled extensively in her twenties and turned to poetry in 1902. While in England with her lover Ada Dwyer Russell, she met American poet Ezra Pound, whose influence as an imagist and fierce critic of Lowell's work would prove essential to her poetry. In 1912, only two years after publishing her first poem in *The Atlantic Monthly*, Lowell produced *A Dome of Many-Coloured Glass,* her debut volume of poems. In addition to such collections of her own poems as *Sword Blades and Poppy Seed* (1914) and *Men, Women, and Ghosts* (1916), Lowell published translations of 8th century Chinese poet Li Tai-po and, at the time of her death, had been working on a biography of English Romantic John Keats.

A Note from the Publisher

Spanning many genres, from non-fiction essays to literature classics to children's books and lyric poetry, Mint Edition books showcase the master works of our time in a modern new package. The text is freshly typeset, is clean and easy to read, and features a new note about the author in each volume. Many books also include exclusive new introductory material. Every book boasts a striking new cover, which makes it as appropriate for collecting as it is for gift giving. Mint Edition books are only printed when a reader orders them, so natural resources are not wasted. We're proud that our books are never manufactured in excess and exist only in the exact quantity they need to be read and enjoyed.

bookfinity™

Discover more of your favorite classics with Bookfinity™.

- Track your reading with custom book lists.
- Get great book recommendations for your personalized Reader Type.
- Add reviews for your favorite books.
- AND MUCH MORE!

Visit **bookfinity.com** and take the fun Reader Type quiz to get started.

Enjoy our classic and modern companion pairings!

Bookfinity is a registered trademark of Ingram Book Group LLC. © 2023 Bookfinity. All rights reserved.

Printed in the USA
CPSIA information can be obtained
at www.ICGtesting.com
JSHW021416160824
R13664500001B/R136645PG68134JSX00008B/15

9 781513 295862